THE SPACE THE DESERT CREATES

THE SPACE THE DESERT CREATES

The Long Way to Myself in the Australian Outback

By

REBECCA KNUDSON

Published by Desert Sky Publishing

ISBN: 979-8-9957704-0-4 (Paperback)
ISBN: 979-8-9957704-1-1 (Hardcover)
ISBN: 979-8-9957704-2-8 (eBook)

Published by Desert Sky Publishing

Illustrations: pikbest.com

This book is a work of nonfiction. All events and experiences described are true to the best of the author's knowledge.

Printed in the United States of America

For my family—
who loved me through the mess of it,
and showed patience when it was
hard to understand.

And for anyone standing at the edge
of something scary—
choose growth.
It's worth it.

A portion of the proceeds from this book will be donated to The Kangaroo Sanctuary—an incredible organization dedicated to rescuing and caring for kangaroos.

This place holds a special meaning in my journey, and I'm honored to support the work they do.

To learn more or make a donation, please visit:
https://kangaroosanctuary.com/

The Kangaroo Sanctuary
PO Box 4921
Alice Springs, NT 0871
Australia

THE RED EARTH ITINERARY: A TIMELINE OF DEPARTURE AND RETURN

The Departure | June 2023

- **5th:** Traded the familiar for a one-way ticket to the unknown.
- **9th:** Touched down in the Red Centre; Alice Springs officially becomes home.
- **13th–14th:** Met "Dimples," my dusty chariot, and stepped into my first classroom at Larapinta Primary.

The Wild Awakening | June — August 2023

- **24th:** My first night in a swag, sleeping under a ceiling of infinite stars at Rainbow Valley.
- **28th:** A first visit to the Kangaroo Sanctuary—a spark of love for the roos begins to flicker.
- **July 27th:** Four-wheel driving through Ross River; learning to navigate a landscape as rugged as my own spirit.
- **Aug 20th:** Returning to the swag at Rainbow Valley; the desert is starting to feel like an old friend.

The Deep Outback | September — October 2023

- **Sept 13th:** Moved into my donga—finding peace and independence within four small metal walls.
- **Sept 18th:** Brad arrives in the Outback; sharing the red earth before his October departure.
- **Sept 24th:** Trip to Uluru.
- **Sept 30th:** Trip to Darwin and Litchfield National Park.
- **Oct 5th:** Another night of swag camping somewhere out bush.
- **Oct 11th (11:11):** A message from the Kangaroo Sanctuary—a sign, a whisper, and a life-changing call.
- **Oct 14th:** Officially started my work at the Sanctuary.

- **Nov 6th:** Witnessed my first kangaroo release—learning the ultimate act of love is letting go.
- **Nov 29th:** First snake encounter—a sharp reminder of the wild's beautiful, dangerous edge.
- **Dec 18th:** Left the Outback to visit the life I left behind.
- **Jan 24th:** Returned to Australia—no longer a visitor, but someone who belongs to the red earth.

The Deepening Roots | February — May 2024

- **Feb 16th:** A second snake encounter—the wild is no longer a novelty, but a neighbor I've learned to respect.
- **Feb 19th:** Swag camping at Ellery Creek Big Hole—finding sanctuary in cool water and ancient stone.
- **March 23rd:** Witnessed the Todd River flow for the second time... one more and legend says I may never leave Alice.
- **April 6th:** The Great Ocean Road with Amy—seeing the edge of the continent before returning to its red heart.
- **April 25th:** Babysitting kangaroos on a movie set—a reminder life here is never ordinary.
- **April 25th:** Saying goodbye to Penny Fairweather—closing a chapter of my Australian home.
- **May:** The Finke Desert Race—feeling the roar and dust of the Outback's ultimate adrenaline rush.

The Final Release | June — July 2024

- **June:** Stood in my classroom at Larapinta for the last time, saying goodbye to the faces that helped me find my own.
- **June:** Accepted a position back home as a district behavior coach at the school where I taught for 20 years.
- **June 28th:** Final day at the Kangaroo Sanctuary—one last release, watching a life I nurtured bound into the wild, just as I am about to do.
- **July 2nd:** Said goodbye to the Outback—leaving the red earth behind, but carrying its dust in my soul forever.

The Story Continues | June — August 2026

- Returning to the Outback—road-tripping dusty tracks with Penny Fairweather, chasing the red horizon once more.

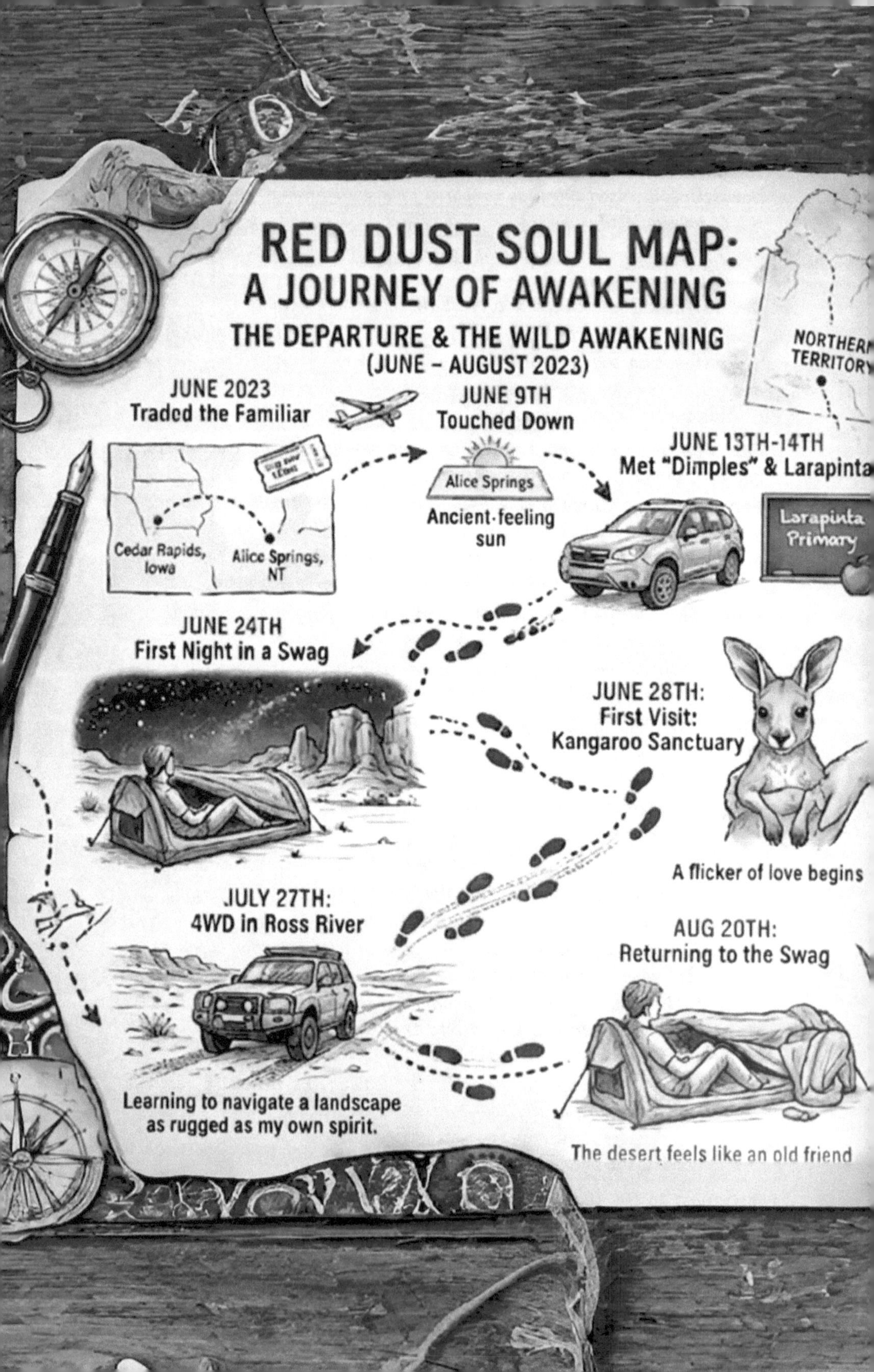

RED DUST SOUL MAP:
A JOURNEY OF AWAKENING
THE DEPARTURE & THE WILD AWAKENING
(JUNE – AUGUST 2023)
NORTHERN TERRITORY
JUNE 2023
Traded the Familiar
JUNE 9TH
Touched Down
JUNE 13TH-14TH
Met "Dimples" & Larapinta
Alice Springs
Ancient-feeling sun
Cedar Rapids, Iowa
Alice Springs, NT
Larapinta Primary
JUNE 24TH
First Night in a Swag
JUNE 28TH:
First Visit:
Kangaroo Sanctuary
A flicker of love begins
JULY 27TH:
4WD in Ross River
AUG 20TH:
Returning to the Swag
Learning to navigate a landscape
as rugged as my own spirit.
The desert feels like an old friend

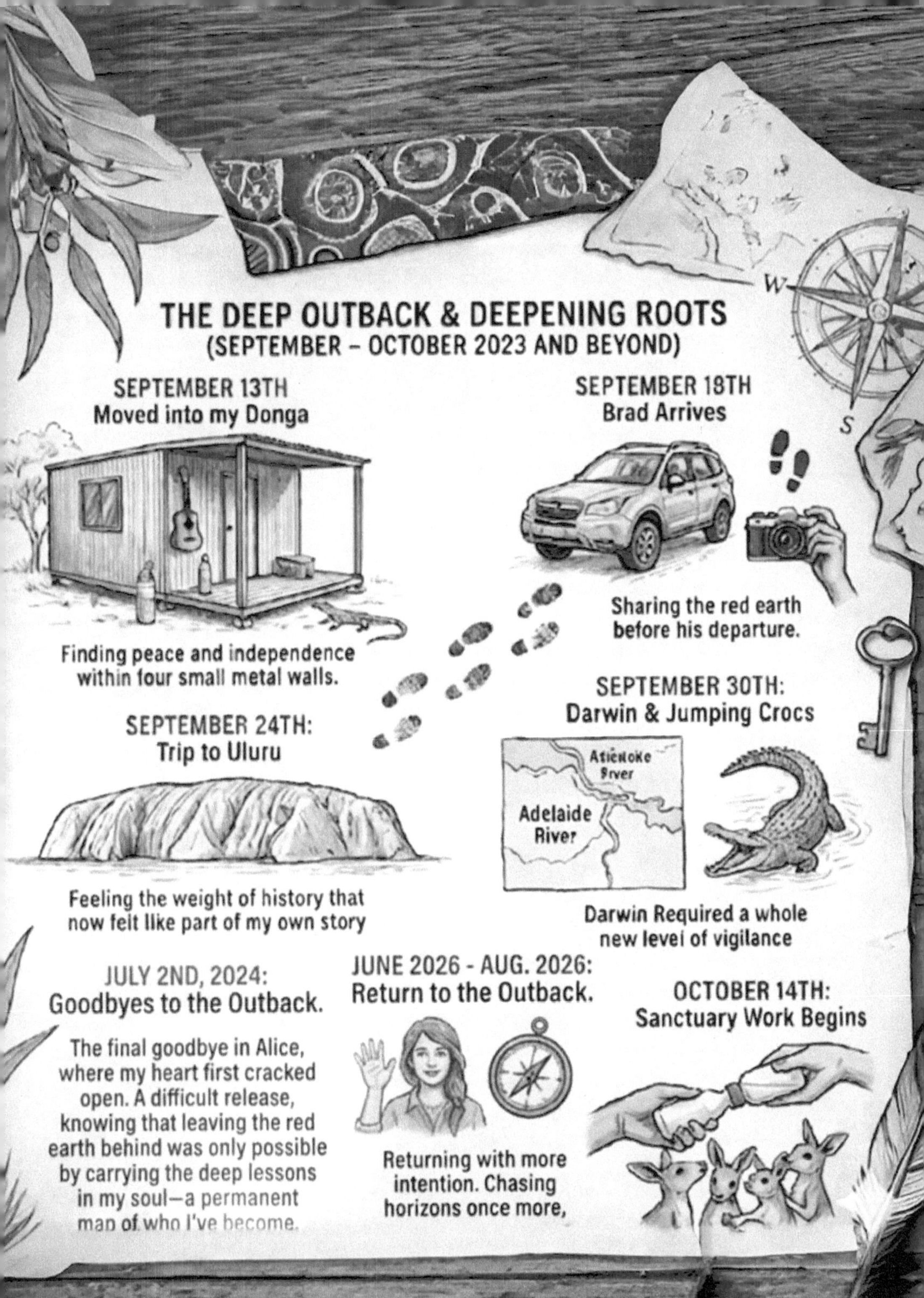

THE DEEP OUTBACK & DEEPENING ROOTS
(SEPTEMBER – OCTOBER 2023 AND BEYOND)
SEPTEMBER 13TH
Moved into my Donga
Finding peace and independence within four small metal walls.
SEPTEMBER 24TH:
Trip to Uluru
Feeling the weight of history that now felt like part of my own story
JULY 2ND, 2024:
Goodbyes to the Outback.
The final goodbye in Alice, where my heart first cracked open. A difficult release, knowing that leaving the red earth behind was only possible by carrying the deep lessons in my soul—a permanent map of who I've become.
SEPTEMBER 18TH
Brad Arrives
Sharing the red earth before his departure.
SEPTEMBER 30TH:
Darwin & Jumping Crocs
Atichoke River
Adelaide River
Darwin Required a whole new level of vigilance
JUNE 2026 - AUG. 2026:
Return to the Outback.
Returning with more intention. Chasing horizons once more,
OCTOBER 14TH:
Sanctuary Work Begins
W
S

CONTENTS

PROLOGUE

The desert is quiet in a way that makes you hear yourself.

Not the surface thoughts — the grocery lists, the lesson plans, the bills, the endless to-do lists. The deeper voice. The one that had been steady and patient for years.

Now I am standing in a place where nothing looks familiar, sounds recognizable, or carries a scent I know. Red dirt settles over everything in a fine layer of dust. The sky stretches open. There are no streetlights. No steady traffic hum. No well-known distractions.

Only space.

I thought coming here would feel adventurous. Brave. Exciting.

What it feels like is stripped down — as if everything unnecessary has fallen away, leaving only the questions I carried with me.

Out here, the voice I tried to hush grows clearer.

It isn't asking me to abandon my life. It isn't suggesting what I built was wrong. It is asking a question more unsettling.

Is this all there is?

When the children are grown and the routines are steady, who are you becoming?

Have you confused comfort with calling?

What else might be waiting if you stepped beyond what you already know you can do?

I left behind a husband I love. Grown children who no longer need me in the same way. A classroom I taught in for twenty years. From the outside, nothing was broken. Nothing demanded fixing.

But the voice was never about what was broken.

It was about what was still possible.

Standing here now, thousands of miles from home, I can't tell if I've made the bravest decision of my life — or the most reckless.

The desert doesn't answer.

It simply waits.

And in the waiting, I begin to understand: This was never about geography. It was about listening.

This is the story of what happened when I finally did.

CHAPTER 1:
MY STORY

What makes someone pack their life into two suitcases and leave behind everything they know and love to fly across the world to a country they've never seen?

The house was quiet the night before I left. My suitcases stood by the door, heavier than the weight limit allowed, as if they understood what they were carrying. In the morning, I had a harder time than expected when I said goodbye to my two dogs, Ozzie and Birdie. Ozzie trembled, confused by the suitcases and the disruption, sensing something was different but not understanding what. Birdie, on the other hand, darted around with her usual joy, dropping her ball at my feet, convinced this was another ordinary day meant for play. One anxious, one blissfully unaware.

Before getting into the car, I knelt and pulled each of them close, pressing my face into their fur and breathing them in as if I could store the scent of them for later. I whispered I loved them, my voice steady, although my heart wasn't, already feeling the ache of missing them before I pulled out of the driveway.

We began the long drive to Texas, where I would say goodbye to my girls and board the plane that would carry me across the world. I remember resting my hand on the console as the miles slipped by, feeling reckless and strangely calm. Excitement buzzed beneath my skin. So did guilt. I was saying goodbye to a life I loved and turning a page to a new chapter.

My journey wasn't about travel, but rather about stepping beyond every comfort zone I carefully built and about trusting that subtle inner voice that kept whispering, *There's more for you than this.*

I didn't know how much Australia would change me — only what lay beneath the surface could not stay the same. A shy restlessness had settled into my days, a sense I was moving through a life that looked full on the outside but felt smaller on the inside. I couldn't have imagined how completely it would reshape not only the way I teach, but the way I see myself... and the world.

This is the story of what happened when I finally listened.

It's a story about responding to that voice, taking a leap when staying would have been easier, and challenging myself in ways I never thought possible. My quest is about stepping into the unknown, leaving behind the known patterns of my life, and choosing growth over comfort.

But it's also about learning to let go — forgiving myself and others, finding beauty in places I never would have chosen, and discovering sometimes space is what teaches you who you've been all along.

Long before Australia, my story began with imagination — the kind that could turn an ordinary afternoon into something vast.

As a child, I turned the simplest moments into grand adventures. Behind my dad's shed, with the smell of cut grass hanging thick in the air, I sailed imaginary oceans, mapping routes to lands that existed only in my mind.

Other days, I became a forest ranger, leading pretend tours through backyards and alleys, pointing out weeds and beetles as if they were rare discoveries.

Still then, I was searching for something beyond what was in front of me.

As I grew older, my adventures evolved. Curiosity pulled me toward abandoned houses, wondering who once lived there and what those cracked walls had witnessed.

Sometimes, curiosity tipped into teenage recklessness — the thrill of trying to buy alcohol before I was twenty-one or the absolute stupidity of car-surfing down a dusty gravel road.

The details changed, but the pull didn't.

That hunger for the unknown never left me. It simply grew quieter... and more persistent.

It was that same restless curiosity that as time went on, led me to pack my life into two suitcases and fly to the other side of the world.

WHEN ADVENTURE TURNED INTO ROUTINE

In the years leading up to Australia, my journals told a different story — one marked by exhaustion, routine, and a growing, creeping unhappiness.

I was living inside the predictability of my days, doing what I was good at, but no longer sure it was what I was meant to keep doing.

I've come to realize this is how life often unfolds for so many of us—gradually shaped by expectation and responsibility—until one day we pause long enough to notice the distance between the life we're living and the one we once imagined.

In December 2019, I wrote a quote that now feels like a message from my past self:

Be yourself. It's the hardest job you will ever have. If you follow the herd, you will never be heard.

Not long after, I wrote:

I end my week feeling frustrated and burned out. Sometimes it's not the week — it's the day. I'm not sure teaching is the path I should continue to take, yet I know I'm a good teacher. I also have a hard time relaxing and enjoying the moment and always feel like I need to be accomplishing items on my to-do list. I'm lost and confused. What do I want clarity on? You are not your thoughts.

Reading those words now, I don't see weakness.

I see awareness.

I see a woman who was searching — not for a new job, but for a different way to live inside her own life. Someone who felt stuck, burned out, and disconnected from joy. Someone who knew, deep down, something had to change.

Because the question was never: What's wrong?

The question was: Is there more?

WHY AUSTRALIA

Long before Australia was ever a real possibility, it lived quietly in my imagination.

When I was a child, one of my favorite books was *Alexander and the Terrible, Horrible, No Good, Very Bad Day*. I remember sitting cross-legged on the carpet flipping through the pages while Alexander complained about what had gone wrong. By the end of the book, after one disaster after another, Alexander decides he is moving to Australia.

In his mind, Australia was the one place in the world where bad days simply didn't happen.

That idea stuck with me.

As a kid, I imagined Australia as this magical, faraway place where life had to be more adventurous than ordinary life in the Midwest. A place where kangaroos hopped around like neighborhood squirrels, the sky was impossibly blue, and the land stretched out forever in shades of red and gold.

In my mind, Australia felt almost mythical.

It was the place you dream about visiting someday—the way people dream about climbing Mount Everest or sailing around the world. Exciting to imagine, but not something you actually expect to do.

Living there? That seemed about as likely as becoming a professional surfer in the Midwest.

Years later, while wandering through an antique store, I came across an old map of Australia. It wasn't particularly valuable or rare, but a feeling pulled me in. The faded colors. The shape of the continent. The vast empty middle.

Before I knew it, I was carrying the map to the checkout counter.

I framed the map and hung it inside my front door. It quickly became a conversation piece. People would walk in, glance at the wall, and ask, "Why do you have a map of Australia?"

I usually shrugged and made a casual comment like, "Oh, I've always wanted to go there."

But the truth was, every time I walked past that map, it reminded me of the quiet dream that had been sitting in the back of my mind since childhood—one I learned to downplay in conversation, as though keeping it small would protect me from the risk of wanting it too much.

I started to convince myself it was too late anyway—by the time you're nearing fifty, your biggest adventures are behind you, and dreams like that are meant to be let go. You don't change your life in such a big way.

And there were the questions—the ones that never seemed to stop. What would people think? What if I went and couldn't handle the change, the homesickness, and had to come back feeling like I failed? Or worse, what if I went... and didn't love Australia at all—this place I built up in my mind since I was little?

The "what ifs" circled endlessly, which is perhaps why I've always disliked those kinds of questions—the "what ifs" stopped me before I ever began.

Over time, that dream started to feel less like a fantasy and more like a plan I needed to try.

Once I decided I was going to teach in Australia, I faced what I thought would be the hardest question: Where in Australia should I go?

Australia is enormous. There are beaches that stretch for miles, tropical rainforests, massive cities, tiny coastal towns, and the enormous interior desert.

But the decision turned out to be surprisingly simple. The decision didn't come from research. It came from a moment.

One morning while getting ready for work, I reached into the closet to grab my coat. As I turned toward the door, my eyes landed on the framed map hanging by the entryway.

I paused.

Without really thinking about it, my eyes drifted toward the middle of the country — that immense empty space that seemed to take up half the map.

Alice Springs.

I never heard of it before. I knew absolutely nothing about it.

But that moment felt strangely clear.

If I was going to move to Australia, I wasn't going to ease into it with beaches and big cities.

Apparently, I was going straight to the middle of the desert.

Even now, I sometimes wonder if that decision came from bravery... or a complete lack of understanding about what living in the Australian Outback actually meant.

Either way, at that moment standing by my front door, the decision was made.

Alice Springs would be my new home.

When I started telling people I was planning to move to Australia, the reactions were exactly what you might expect. Most people thought it sounded exciting — until I mentioned where I was going.

"Alice Springs?" they would say. "Where's that?"

"It's right in the middle of Australia," I would explain.

Another pause. Usually, a longer one.

"You mean... the desert?"

Yes. The desert.

The way people said *desert* made it sound less like a location and more like a warning.

Some people assumed I meant Sydney or maybe at a location near the beach. Explaining I was moving to the middle of the Australian Outback often deferred the conversation from *That sounds amazing* to *Are you sure that's a good idea?*

The truth was, I wasn't entirely sure it was a good idea.

But it felt right.

Unlike many people who move overseas, I didn't go through a placement company to arrange details. No one helped me find a school. No one organized the visas, housing, flights, or the long list of logistics that come with moving so far away.

Apparently, I decided the easiest way to move to the other side of the world was to do it the hardest way possible.

Once I decided Alice Springs was the place, the real work began.

What I hadn't realized at the time was how complicated it is to move to another country. Finding a teaching position was only one piece of the puzzle. The much bigger challenge was figuring out how to legally live and work in Australia.

At my age, visa options were limited, and it took an enormous amount of research to figure out which visa I might qualify for.

What started as curiosity quickly turned into a full-blown mission.

Every night after school and nearly every weekend, I sat at my computer researching. Hours turned into weeks as I worked my way through government websites, visa requirements, teaching credentials, immigration regulations, and enough online forms to make my eyes cross.

For a time, my browser had so many immigration tabs open I was fairly certain the Australian government was personally monitoring my laptop.

I researched how to obtain an Australian visa.
How to get a teaching license in the Northern Territory.
How to complete background checks.
How to receive clearances to work with children.

I found myself researching how I might buy a car in Alice Springs — a town never seen, in a desert never visited, on a continent on the other side of the planet.

The list seemed endless.

Some nights it felt overwhelming. Other nights it felt thrilling — like slowly piecing together a giant puzzle that might unlock the adventure I dreamed about for years.

And there were the nights when it all felt like too much, when I wanted to give up entirely. It reminded me of starting a diet—the way motivation can feel so strong during the day, only to unravel at night when desserts as simple as ice cream makes you think, *Why not stay the same and make life easier?*

I found myself thinking the same thing: Maybe life would be easier if I stopped pushing myself, if I stayed where I was and let the dream go.

There were many nights I tried to convince myself to quit, coming up with a thousand reasons why it wasn't a good idea. But over time, I began to recognize that voice for what it was—my ego. It was the part of me that wanted to stay safe, avoid discomfort, and protect myself from failure or disappointment.

But that voice wasn't the one leading me toward growth. The quieter voice—the one that didn't shout or panic—was the one worth understanding. It didn't promise ease, but it carried a sense of truth, curiosity, and possibility. I started to understand while the ego tries to keep you comfortable, your inner voice is what moves you forward.

In the middle of all that research, I began reaching out to schools.

I had no idea if anyone would respond.

But my very core kept saying, *Just keep going.*

The moment I spoke with Brenda Jolly, the principal at Larapinta Primary School, I felt this might be the place.

Our first interview took place on a Friday night. I finished a long week of teaching, my hair pulled into a messy bun, and I was operating purely on teacher survival mode.

But the conversation flowed easily from the start.

It didn't feel like a formal interview. It was relaxed — like talking with someone I knew for years. Brenda had a warmth about her that made the idea of moving halfway around the world feel a little less intimidating.

It's hard to explain, but in that moment, it clicked. It felt... established. Like this place so far away might somehow still hold pieces of home.

The feeling reminded me of walking into my parents' house—the same comforting smell, the usual trinkets still sitting on the shelves, the quilt neatly spread across the bed. The little reminders that never change: the old alarm clock, the lamp that turns on with a simple touch, the objects that softly hold years of memories. And the deeper comfort—pulling out childhood toys or playing a favorite game like *Madcap Marathon*, when, for a moment, everything feels exactly as it once was.

That's what it felt like talking to Brenda. A sense of ease, of recognition—like I wasn't stepping into the entirely unknown, but into something that, in its own way, already felt like home.

Before long, it was decided I would teach science at Larapinta Primary.

The dream started to morph into reality.

But even with the job lined up, the mountain of logistics remained. I still had to secure the visa, arrange sponsorship, complete background checks, obtain my Northern Territory teaching license, and navigate all the other requirements that come with moving internationally.

At times, I wished there had been a company specialized in helping teachers through this process — someone who could say, *Here's step one. Here's step two. And step three involves less paperwork.*

But no such company really existed.

So I figured it out one step at a time.

Night after night.
Weekend after weekend.

Each form completed and each email sent brought the dream a little closer to reality.

At some point, another idea began to take shape. Someday, I would love to help other teachers find their way to the Red Centre. Alice Springs is the kind of place that changes people, and there are so many educators who would thrive there if they had a little help navigating the process.

Maybe one day I'll create an easier path.

For now, I'm simply happy to help anyone who asks.

Because I know firsthand how overwhelming the process can feel — and how life-changing the journey can become.

Before I knew it, a place I never heard of a few months earlier — a tiny dot in the middle of the map hanging by my front door — was about to become my new home.

WHEN THE IDEA BECAME REAL

I don't remember the exact moment Australia turned from dream to possibility, but once it did, it took root in a way I couldn't ignore. It was what I thought about when I woke up, what lingered in my mind throughout the day, and what followed me into the silent moments at night when I should have been sleeping.

I found myself checking my email in the middle of the night, knowing with the time difference, messages from Australia would arrive while the rest of my world was still asleep. I didn't want to wait until morning—I wanted to read them the moment they came through, to understand the next step, to keep the momentum going.

It wasn't a passing thought anymore. It had settled in, steady and persistent, becoming a part of me I couldn't push aside.

Journal Entry — 4/23/23

I've stepped into fears I never imagined, and some have turned into sparks of pure excitement. I'm proud of myself for responding to that constant inner hum and taking the leap. This isn't who I've always been—and that makes every step feel alive, like discovering a new part of myself. I'll carry this moment with me, proof of how far I can go when I listen to myself. Beneath it, I wrote down what I hoped might change in me during this journey. Not grand transformations—small shifts.

I hoped to find a little more peace inside my own mind. To worry less and trust life a bit more. To meet new people and unfamiliar places with curiosity instead of caution. I wanted the courage to try challenges that might make me uncomfortable and the grace to laugh at myself when they do.

Mostly, I hoped to slow down long enough to notice the world around me—to appreciate the beauty of nature and remember life doesn't have to be complicated to be meaningful.

At the bottom of the page, I left myself a simple note:

Be ready to let go. Jump in. Grow. You've got this.

THE GOODBYE
6/5/23 — ON THE WAY TO THE AIRPORT

The car was quiet in the way that only happens when too many emotions are sitting in the same space.

Outside, everything looked completely normal. People were driving to work. Gas stations were opening. The world was moving along like any other Monday morning.

But inside the car, my entire life felt like it was being pulled apart.

I was on my way to the airport to move to Australia.

Even saying the words in my head felt surreal.

Part of me was almost vibrating with excitement. After months of research, paperwork, late nights, and more uncertainty than I ever willingly invited into my life, it was finally happening.

I was actually doing this.

Another part of me was absolutely terrified.

My emotions swung wildly between pride and panic. One moment I felt brave — proud of myself for having the strength to chase dreams so big and uncertain. The next moment I wondered if I completely lost my mind.

Who gets on a plane and moves to the other side of the world?

Apparently... I did.

In a hidden place far down inside, I believed there was a reason I was being pulled toward Alice Springs, yet I couldn't fully explain why. A feeling about the desert, about the space, about the unknown, was calling me forward.

I tried to focus on that.

I reminded myself this journey would hold beauty. New experiences. New friendships. Growth I couldn't yet imagine.

There would also be hard days. Lonely nights. Moments when I would question it all.

But I promised myself I would embrace it all.

I would learn. I would grow. I would make the most of this opportunity.

At least, that's what I told myself.

But none of those brave thoughts prepared me for the moment it was time to say goodbye.

SAYING GOODBYE

Leaving was harder than I imagined.

The moment that nearly broke me was saying goodbye to Brad.

We had tried to keep the conversations light in those final moments, the way people do when they're both trying not to fall apart. A few jokes. A few forced smiles.

But the truth sat between us, heavy and unavoidable.

I was leaving.

Not for a week. Not for a vacation.

For a year.

Possibly longer.

I can still see his face at that moment — the way his lip trembled as he tried to hold it together. The way his eyes filled with tears he was clearly fighting to hide.

That was the moment my heart started to break.

Because suddenly, this wasn't merely my dream anymore.

It was also the pain I was causing someone I loved.

The guilt hit me like a wave.

What kind of person leaves the people they love to chase a dream on the other side of the world?

I can still feel that moment — standing there with my suitcase, trying to act strong while everything deep inside me was unraveling, like holding a fragile object I was terrified to drop, knowing that letting go was inevitable.

We hugged longer than usual.

Neither of us wanting to be the one to let go first.

At some point, we had to.

Because planes don't wait for people to finish emotional goodbyes.

When we finally pulled apart, Brad looked at me and said quietly, "Promise me you'll come back."

I nodded, but the truth was I had no idea what the next year would bring.

Then came the hardest part.

Turning around and walking away.

I took a few steps, stopped, and turned back one more time.

Brad was still standing there watching me go.

And that was the moment my heart felt like it was ripping in half.

Because I knew if I walked back to him, I might not get on that plane at all.

So instead, I picked up my suitcase... wiped my eyes... and kept walking.

TWO DAYS LATER — BRISBANE AIRPORT

I sat in the Brisbane airport waiting for my flight to Sydney.

And that's when the emotional weight finally caught up.

The last twenty-four hours had been mentally exhausting. The adrenaline that had carried me through departure had faded, leaving behind a raw mix of grief, fear, exhaustion, and doubt.

I cried harder than I knew I could.

The crying that leaves your chest aching and your eyes swollen.

I sat there staring out the airport window, thinking, *What have I done?*

For a moment, it honestly felt like I was stuck in a bad dream — the kind where you desperately want to wake up and return to the life you know.

The comfortable life.

The safe life.

I never felt so scared.

But in a place beneath the fear — buried under the tears and the guilt — rested another emotion.

Relief.

A quiet, fragile sense of relief I followed through.

I hadn't backed out at the last minute.

It would have been easy to back out.

Very easy.

Instead, I was sitting in an airport in Australia with reddened eyes, a tired heart, and a one-way ticket deeper into the unknown. And yet, it occurred to me I'd taken a leap most wouldn't, made a change braver than I usually believed possible for me.

Bright airport lights. Suitcases rolling across the floor. The hum of travelers moving in every direction.

And me, sitting in the middle of it all, feeling like I stepped outside my own life and was watching it unfold.

I already felt cracked open.

But I reminded myself of something simple.

Bad days happen everywhere.

Even in Australia.

THE BEGINNING

That was the beginning.

The fear.
The tears.
The guilt that sat heavy on my heart.
The fragile courage it took to keep moving forward.

I didn't realize what was waiting for me in the Red Centre.

I didn't know about the red dirt that would cling to everything.
The kangaroos that would appear when I least expected them.
The friendships that would form.
The heartbreaks that would come.
Or the quiet, powerful ways the desert would stretch me and reshape the person I thought I was.

All of that was still ahead.

But in the middle of the fear and the tears...

I said yes anyway.

With shaking hands.

And a full heart.

And that yes changed everything.

CHAPTER 2:
I'VE ARRIVED

6/9/23 — THE FIRST NIGHT

I arrived in Alice Springs exhausted, emotionally wrung out, and running purely on adrenaline. When I saw Brenda, the principal of Larapinta Primary, standing there to greet me, relief crashed over me so suddenly my knees nearly buckled. I walked straight into her arms and held on longer than I meant to — as if letting go would change everything, pulling me back to the very start— the long nights of paperwork, the hard decisions, and the unbearable partings.

She looked at me with concern and asked if I was okay. I told her the truth — I was so relieved to be here finally, and I felt like I experienced every emotion possible in the last two days of travel.

What I didn't know yet was this was only the very start of what my nervous system would have to endure. Fear. Terror. Loneliness — the kind that hits fast and lodges itself in your chest.

My first real lesson didn't happen in a classroom. It happened my very first night — alone — in an Airbnb.

That night would change me in ways I didn't expect.

In my journal, I wrote:

The last twenty-four hours are not moments I want to relive, but it was a necessary step in my journey. To truly understand others' situations, you must put yourself in their shoes.

The Airbnb smelled sour and damp, was visibly filthy, and immediately made me feel unsafe. The carpet was stained and sticky under my shoes. The air smelled like damp fabric and old food had soaked into the walls. A panic rose in me I didn't recognize — sharp, physical, uncontrollable. Cobwebs hung in every corner. A towel hung from the ceiling to separate the toilet from the laundry and kitchen area. That was the "private bathroom."

Looking back, part of the reason this experience felt so terrifying was because I had never traveled on my own before. After nearly twenty-five years of marriage, I had never been away from my husband for more than a few days. All of that, combined with my senses on overdrive and lack of sleep, created a storm I wasn't prepared to handle. I can see that if I returned now, with more confidence and familiarity with travel, the experience would feel different—but I would never choose to stay somewhere where the door didn't lock and hosts entered unannounced and uninvited.

I was exhausted and overwhelmed. I missed Brad and everything about home. I pulled out my phone and stared at the last message he had sent me. I wanted to text him, but I didn't know what to say. I wanted to sleep, but I was scared and couldn't. I started to panic in a way I never had before. I felt more alone than I ever had — not physically alone, but emotionally untethered. At one moment, I whispered to myself, "What have I done?" The thought was almost unbearable.

I was cold, hungry, and a little delirious. The walls were paper thin. It sounded like cars were going to drive straight through the room. I heard people screaming and yelling throughout the night. The owners entered my room three different times without warning. Each time, whatever fragile sense of safety I managed to build collapsed. I was terrified. I stayed under the blankets, too scared and cold to get up and use the bathroom.

I felt trapped — not by locked doors, but by my own fear.

The adventure I thought I was chasing had dissolved into fear. That first night took something out of me — it left me jumpy and uneasy.

As awful as it was, it forced me to confront thoughts I never fully understood. There are people who live with fear every single night — and still show up the next morning expected to learn, to work, to function as if nothing is wrong.

The last twenty-four hours were terrifying — but maybe that terror was the onset of understanding.

The next morning, I shared a raw update with friends and family. I didn't sugarcoat it. I told them the truth — the first twenty-four hours had been awful. I never felt so scared or so alone. I questioned my decision and begged my family to book a flight home for me.

I wrote about the screaming, the sirens, and the host entering my room unannounced. About how I barely slept. About how my eyes were swollen from crying and how I was still wearing the same clothes from the airport when Brenda came to pick me up.

And then, unexpectedly — rescue.

The staff at Larapinta Primary stepped in immediately. A teacher opened her home to me while she was on holiday in Perth. Her house felt like a palace. After that night, a couch and a clean towel felt luxurious.

My assistant principal picked me up, gave me a tour of Alice Springs, bought me coffee and toast, and helped me run errands. Slowly, I felt human again.

I wrote I never wanted to experience a night like that again, yet it taught me important lessons— how much we take for granted a warm, safe place to sleep. That night gave me a powerful understanding of what so many people live with every day.

I ended my update with a line from *Alexander and the Terrible, Horrible, No Good, Very Bad Day*, reminding myself of a simple truth I wasn't quite ready to accept — some days are like that... even in Australia.

LOST IN TRANSLATION

That night was only the first of many lessons Australia would teach me.

Some lessons came with humor.

At the grocery store, I asked my friend Mullins, "What's a chook?"

She looked at me like I was ridiculous. "Chicken," she said.

Then there was the day a Year-4 student asked me for a rubber.

"A rubber?" I repeated, instantly horrified.

The student quickly corrected herself in front of the American teacher. "An eraser."

I was also told if I went outside at night, I needed to carry a torch so I didn't step on a snake. At the time, I was still translating everything in my head, so I immediately pictured an actual torch — like fire, flames, scenes out of *Raiders of the Lost Ark*. In my mind, I wasn't stepping outside... I was preparing for battle against snakes in every direction. It took me a minute (and probably a slightly confused look) to realize they meant a flashlight. A normal, everyday flashlight.

Those moments started my growing list of Australian slang — proof we almost needed a translator to survive daily conversation in this rural corner of the world. (See the end of the book for translations... because I had to start writing them down to keep up.)

On my first day in a tiny classroom, a first grader looked up at me with wide, curious eyes.

"Miss, why do you talk funny?"

I laughed. "I don't talk funny. You do."

That's when the ice cracked — although I still had no idea what I was doing.

I quickly learned Australia had its own language, its own current, and its own way of throwing me off balance — sometimes painfully, sometimes beautifully.

I arrived — but I was nowhere near settled.

And the real journey was only getting started.

CHAPTER 3

THE UPS AND DOWNS OF MY FIRST WEEK

My first week in Alice Springs felt like a lifetime compressed into a handful of days. Every emotion showed up — sometimes within the same hour. I quickly learned settling into a new country isn't linear. It jerks, dips, and climbs without warning.

Journal Entry — 6/11/23

I would call today a win —though it began in tears. I cried for home. I cried from exhaustion. I cried because my body and mind still hadn't caught up to where I was. I wasn't sleeping well, and the dry air had started to steal my voice. I couldn't tell if I was getting sick or if my body was reacting to the desert.

I forced myself to say yes —though every part of me wanted to retreat. I went to lunch with Brenda, Jackie, and two of their friends. At first, I felt awkward, but once I loosened up, I laughed more than I expected.

Lunch turned into my first real Australian language lesson.

A fanny pack is absolutely not a word you say casually in Australia.

Supper means a snack after dinner.

Britches are underwear.

A purse is a wallet.

And a bag is what I would call a purse.

I tried to store all of it in my already-overloaded brain, hoping I wouldn't embarrass myself too badly in the future.

After lunch, I wandered over to visit my neighbor, Daphine — Daph. I sat with her, her partner, and a friend. During that time, I mentioned my husband. They burst out laughing and said, "Do you know we're all lesbians here?"

We all laughed. It was one of those moments that reminded me how quickly connection forms when you stop trying to manage how you're perceived.

They helped me brainstorm housing options and later invited me to supper at a Vietnamese restaurant. The food was incredible. We shared drinks, stories, and laughs. Daph told me most people who come to Alice Springs only plan to visit and somehow end up staying.

That was the first time I felt the shift — a softening, a sense maybe I could belong here.

My lesson that day was simple: Go anyway. Even when you feel awkward. Even when you feel unsure. That's where change begins.

Journal Entry — 6/13/23

Today, I felt steady. Stronger than a few days ago. After the events I went through, I realized a powerful truth—every single time I pushed myself outside my comfort zone, I learned something. About life. About people. About myself.

Sitting there I felt in awe of this place. The sounds of nature. The clean desert air. There was a sense a shift bigger was happening at the center of who I am. In five days, something buried within me stretched — uncomfortably, but undeniably.

Daph dropped me off at the Stuart Highway, where I met Allen, the man who helped me buy my car before I arrived in Australia. Within minutes of meeting, he said, "We'll take the ute to go get your license."

I nodded like I understood... but internally, I had no idea what he was talking about. My eyes actually scanned around, trying to spot this "ute," and for some reason, my brain landed on the image of a donkey. A donkey. Standing there on the side of the Stuart Highway, ready to take us into town.

Allen must have caught the confusion on my face because he started laughing. "I think you call it a pick-up truck in America," he said.

He spent hours with me helping me get my license and registering my car. It was close to three hours of waiting, paperwork, and stories.

Allen told me he had only stopped in Alice because he ran out of money and that was forty-eight years ago. Now he owns a date farm and ships dates worldwide. He hires local artists to design his date boxes every year so the community can be part of his business.

Then he put the plates on my car. And the next thing I knew, I was driving on the opposite side of the road, heart pounding at every roundabout.

Meet Dimples — hail-damaged, slightly crooked, and suddenly my lifeline.

LEFT-SIDE-OF-THE-ROAD DRIVING

Driving on the left side of the road was, without question, the hardest thing I have ever done. Every instinct about driving was suddenly wrong. I found myself planning my route to school so I could avoid right turns altogether — because they were basically left turns in disguise.

Even the simplest tasks turned into challenges. Crossing the street on foot meant looking the opposite way than I had before. I learned this the hard way — on my very first day in Alice Springs, I nearly got smashed by a massive truck when my brain instinctively looked the wrong direction. Somehow, I managed to leap clear, heart pounding, praying the driver didn't think I was some clueless American street hazard. Lesson learned: Never underestimate how strongly your habits are wired.

Getting in and out of a car was confusing, too. I can't count how many times I climbed into the wrong side of my own car. Or the time I slid into the driver's seat of someone else's car without thinking, only for them to raise an eyebrow and ask, "Do you want to drive?" Nothing screams "American outsider" quite like fumbling on the wrong side of a car in front of someone who has done this their entire life. Each of those moments was small on its own, but together they chipped away at my confidence, reminding me over and over again I was out of my element.

Not that driving on the left side was hard enough, Alice Springs had a roundabout with five exits. Five! This felt like the universe's ultimate challenge. I'm embarrassed to admit several times I kept circling, trying to figure out which exit was mine, reciting the quote from *National Lampoon's Vacation* out loud: "Look, kids! Big Ben!" as if doing so would somehow make the exit appear. In those moments, I would half laugh, half panic, hoping no one behind me noticed I accidentally turned a roundabout into my own personal orbit.

For weeks, I only stopped when absolutely necessary, hands locked tight on the wheel. Music was out of the question—my brain had one job and one job only: Stay on the left side of the road. Every drive felt like a test I hadn't studied for, with stakes way too high to wing it. I was hyper-aware of everything—every turn, every car, every movement—quietly coaching myself the whole time: left side, left side, left side.

Each drive was exhausting, mentally and emotionally. I knew one wrong move could ruin the day—or at the very least, confirm every stereotype about clueless American drivers. Even pulling into a parking spot became a full mental exercise: Which side do I check first? Which way does the car swing? Am I really about to risk turning on the radio? I felt like a beginner all over again, stripped of the ease and confidence that once felt automatic.

And then, slowly, things shifted. The stops grew smoother. The turns lost their edge. I caught myself letting my mind wander, even humming along to the radio like I wasn't operating heavy machinery in reverse-world traffic. At some point, it clicked. Driving didn't just feel manageable—it felt fun. Like being sixteen again, cruising around for no reason at all, just because I could—half expecting someone to look over and think, *Wow… she just figured it out.*

That sense of freedom came back in the most unexpected place, on the opposite side of the world, on the opposite side of the road.

In fact, I became so attached to my car, Dimples I looked into the cost of having her shipped back to the United States. I went from gripping the wheel in fear to not wanting to let her go. In the end, I decided having a steering wheel on the right side probably wouldn't be the best option for me — it was confusing enough as it was, unless I was planning to start delivering the mail.

Looking back, what once felt impossible slowly became second nature. In between the wrong turns, the missed exits, and the near truck incident, I realized I was no longer simply learning how to drive again — I was learning how to adapt, laugh at myself, and find confidence in places that once made me question everything.

THE WRONG SCHOOL, THE RIGHT LESSON

My first official day at school came with a classic Becky moment. I went to the wrong school.

I confidently walked into the Lutheran school next door before realizing my mistake. Once I made it to Larapinta Primary, my first real impression was — wow.

How could children feel so different from what I knew, yet so recognizably the same?

The differences stood out immediately.

Every student wore a uniform at the school. In America, kids all have different clothing, which immediately sets the tone—who has new clothes, which name brands they wear, and which kids wear the same clothes almost every day. Some students are instantly singled out or made fun of, a harsh reality that feels unavoidable. In Australia, however, every student wore a uniform, and it was worn with a sense of pride. When seen out in the community, students wore it proudly, and when you saw other kids in the same uniform, it was comforting and affirming to know they belonged to the same school. No one's outfit made them a target or defined them. The focus was on learning, playing, and being together rather than on appearances.

At Larapinta Primary, kindergarten through sixth grade played together on the same playground, and somehow, it worked. I can't imagine young kids and older kids sharing a playground in America. There might be smooth moments, but I often picture small children being trampled by bigger students playing rowdy football or simply being overshadowed while trying to interact with friends.

Most American kids have their heads down, scrolling on phones, missing the chance to play freely. In Australia, the same massive playground accommodated all grades at once, with music areas, construction pods, footy fields, and netball courts giving kids space to run, explore, and connect. Students had time to play before school and during long breaks. The routines were strong, the expectations clear, and the sense of community solid.

Cell phones made the difference sharper. In America, life without them is unimaginable. Students are constantly distracted; although phones are supposed to stay in lockers, they find ways to sneak them into pockets or bags, texting under the teacher's nose while pretending to listen. Drama, gossip, and social media flare-ups dominate lunch and spill into the afternoon, creating constant reminders and disruptions.

In Australia, there were no cell phones at school, and lunch was an entirely different experience. Students sat on blankets under the shade of playground trees, opening lunchboxes full of fresh fruit, sandwiches, and homemade snacks. Teachers joined in, tossing down their own blankets and sharing meals while chatting with kids. I remember one afternoon hearing a group of students quietly singing a song they had learned in music class, while a teacher discussed the learning planned for the afternoon. Later, I watched another group building a fort with planks in the construction area while others played footy nearby, and everyone somehow gave each other space and respect. Kids ran, laughed, played, and connected. No screens, no scrolling, no social media drama before class. Childhood felt alive, united, and grounded in simple, meaningful routines.

Even the lunches themselves told a story. In America, it's common to see kids carrying full-size bags of Cheetos or other junk food as their lunch, rarely including fresh fruits or vegetables. Much of the food is packaged or processed. In Australia, lunches were healthy and fresh. Candy was strictly for home.

The culture extended beyond playgrounds and lunch. At Larapinta Primary, kids spoke a mix of languages — Arrernte, Luritja, Pitjantjatjara, and Warlpiri, among others. Ancient, beautiful languages lived and breathed in the community, and hearing them made me realize how sheltered my understanding of history and language had been. American schools, while diverse, often feel more monolingual and culturally segmented, with less of this richness visible in everyday life.

I was blown away and wondered if I could ever go back to teaching in an American school, where social pressures, technology distractions, and fragmented playgrounds seem to steal away so much of what makes childhood feel whole.

JOYRIDES TO NOWHERE

Not everything in Alice Springs was easy to understand.

One of the most challenging realities to wrap my head around was the level of crime, especially car theft. Young people would steal cars, racing them through town, hanging out of windows, chasing adrenaline or attention, and abandon the vehicles — often setting them on fire two or three days later. Sometimes my morning drive to school turned into an impromptu "crime tour." I'd pass the same streets I'd driven countless times, scanning for remnants of the night before: smashed windshields, bent metal, tire marks crisscrossing the red dirt, and the occasional car patiently waiting for its fiery fate.

It became a strange routine — a mix of morbid fascination and disbelief. I'd wonder, "How long until this car goes from stolen joyride to smoking pile of metal?" Often, it took two or three days before someone decided it was time. One morning, I caught myself timing it mentally, like some grim race: car abandoned, chaos settled, fire ignited — all while I sipped my coffee and tried not to think too hard about the absurdity of it.

I struggled to understand it. Why destroy it completely? What were they trying to prove? What pain sat underneath that behavior? I didn't have answers — and honestly, I still don't. But I knew this was part of the story of this place — complex, layered, and fundamentally human. Life in Alice Springs had a rawness to it: danger, recklessness, humor, and resilience all coexisting in the red dust.

As the sun rose over the MacDonnell Ranges, painting the sky pink and gold, the red earth seemed to glow. Endless skies stretched above jagged cliffs, and the calmness of the desert made the town's chaos feel far away. During that moment, I realized

Alice Springs was more than its wild edges — it was a place that could take your breath away and silently steal your heart.

6/18/23 — RED DIRT, ANCIENT VOICES

Sunday night settled in heavily. It was Father's Day in America, but not in Australia. I talked to my parents for the first time since arriving and wished, with an ache I couldn't shake, that I could hug my dad. And Brad.

That weekend, we had a teacher in-service and were given a private tour by two Elders from the community. Taking in their stories was powerful and heartbreaking.

They spoke about respect. About being heard. About how respect is taught and how fully it matters.

Alice Springs is not solely Alice Springs — to the local Arrernte people, it is Mparntwe (m-barn-tweh), a place alive with stories, spirits, and creation. Walking across the red dirt I felt a gentle awe.

The land itself is a guide, mapped by the Dreaming tracks that trace the paths of ancestral beings across sandstone and riverbeds. The Yeperenye (yep-uh-ren-yay), the caterpillars, are said to be the major creative ancestors of Mparntwe, shaping the land as they traveled. But they were not alone. Wild dogs, euros, kangaroos, and other beings also left their mark, carving the ridges, gaps, and valleys I now tried to navigate with careful, respectful steps, feeling a gentle sense of wonder.

Everywhere I looked, I felt the weight of thousands of years of history. The red dirt beneath my boots, the winding dry riverbeds, the ridges and cliffs — they were more than landscape; they were living memory.

I wanted to understand the stories hidden in the land, to know what each rock and riverbank had witnessed. But I had to accept these stories are not mine to tell, and I do not have the knowledge to share them with the respect they deserve.

Still, being here made my chest tighten in amazement. I felt small, humbled, and connected all at once — a visitor trying to hold the enormity of this place in my heart, knowing I could only glimpse its depth. Without fully knowing the stories, I sensed the power, the presence, and the pulse of Mparntwe.

We visited sacred sites around Alice Springs. At Anzac Hill, one of the Elders spoke in Arrernte so the spirits and ancestors would know why we were there. "If the spirits don't know your business," she explained, "they can become upset."

It made me realize how firmly anchored this land is to story, spirit, and history. Not a place — but a living presence.

That night, loneliness returned — faint but persistent. Evenings were the hardest. My family was asleep when I got home from work. I thought about my dog Ozzie and how much he must miss me. My heart ached. Some nights, I needed to close my journal before the tears blurred the page.

Journal Entry — 6/20/23

Today was better. Teaching felt smoother. After school, we had a staff meeting, and it was organized, purposeful, thoughtful.

Brenda told the staff how courageous I was to come halfway around the world to teach. Hearing that said out loud startled me. She was right. I was courageous. And I was growing.

I missed Brad. I missed my kids. I missed Ozzie and Birdie. Some days, the missing felt physical — a tightness in my chest that didn't ease. But I kept reminding myself — this journey would be worth it.

My first week taught me this: Growth is messy. Courage is uncomfortable. Adventure is far more exhausting than it looks from the outside.

And the moments that keep you going often arrive discreetly.

I was still scared. Still homesick. Still unsure.

But I was also becoming someone slightly braver than the woman who had stepped off that plane.

And I was slowly starting to grasp that arrival and belonging are not the same thing.

CHAPTER 4:
PENNY FAIRWEATHER: A LIVING FAIRY TALE

There are some people so central to a journey they require their own entry point into the story. For me, that person was Penny. I haven't mentioned her yet, but to tell the story of my time in Australia without her would be to leave out the heart of it. She became one of the anchors of my life—inspiring me, challenging me, and helping me grow in ways I never expected. Even her name, Penny Fairweather, feels like a character lifted from a fairy tale, as if she stepped out of a story rather than into my real life.

I was introduced to Penny through a friend of a friend, and I had the privilege of living with her from July until my donga was ready in September. What I didn't know was how fully she would influence the way I experienced Australia — and myself within it.

Penny has lived a life shaped by movement and risk — one chapter rarely staying still for long. She worked as a remote nurse in communities scattered across Australia, each experience adding depth and perspective to her already-expansive life. Her knowledge is vast, and her vocabulary often made me pause — unsure whether

I'd heard a word I didn't know, an accent I couldn't catch, or an uniquely Australian expression.

One afternoon, we were sitting on her couch, the ceiling fan humming lazily above us. Late light filtered through the windows, turning the dust in the air gold. I cradled a warm mug between my palms. Penny had her tea balanced confidently on the armrest beside her. Roxie, her dog, lay curled in her small bed near the door, one eye half-open, as if supervising the entire exchange.

Penny reached beside her and picked up several neatly typed pages, slightly creased at the corners. "I made you a copy," she said, handing them to me. It felt oddly official — like my first assignment. My first lesson.

As she took a slow sip of tea, she began walking me through the comparisons she'd outlined between Aboriginal and Western cultural patterns. She described Indigenous worldviews as deeply relational — spirituality woven into everyday life, time understood as circular and tied to natural cycles, humans carrying responsibility for maintaining balance with the land.

By contrast, she explained, Western systems often separate the sacred from the ordinary, measure time linearly, and emphasize growth, ownership, and individual achievement.

She spoke thoughtfully, not as someone delivering a lecture, but as someone inviting me to look again.

What struck me wasn't one way was entirely right and the other entirely wrong. It was the possibility the way I'd been taught to see the world wasn't the only way. That maybe relationships are more important than getting things done. That you can respect and care for something while still taking action.

Those conversations unsettled me — in the best way. They forced me to question how I had been taught to see the world.

Penny didn't offer information; she challenged assumptions I hadn't realized I was carrying.

Penny is, quite simply, a force — and she's nearly eighty. She fills her days with purpose — tending her garden, arguing cheerfully with her feisty chihuahua Roxie, volunteering across town, meeting friends for morning tea (or afternoon tea or any excuse for tea). She is fiercely independent, sometimes stubborn to a fault. If she believes she's right, you better arrive with evidence, or good luck convincing her otherwise.

One of her greatest loves is off-roading in her massive truck. I'll never forget the day she drove to the top of Tin Can Hill. The Four-Wheel Drive Club gathered at the bottom, engines rumbling, a few raised eyebrows as Penny positioned her truck.

"You sure you don't want someone to guide you?" one man called out.

She waved him off.

She didn't only climb that hill — she crawled up it steadily, engine growling, refusing to let anyone take the lead. The truck tilted at angles that made my stomach tighten. But she never hesitated.

When she reached the top, she stepped out calmly, as if she had parked at the grocery store.

Living with Penny during that transitional season of my life felt significant in ways I didn't yet have language for. I was unraveling old versions of myself, questioning long-held beliefs, stepping into unfamiliar territory. And here was this older woman — not soft, not sentimental — but deeply alive, intellectually sharp, and entirely unafraid to live on her own terms.

Penny's fearlessness, curiosity, and no-bullshit honesty continue to challenge me. Not everyone is lucky enough to meet someone like Penny at exactly the moment they need her.

She is fierce, thoughtful, and unapologetically herself — a reminder that living fully has very little to do with age and more to do with boldness.

Penny and me at the top of Tin Can Hill:
Notice the tin can at the top of the pole.

CHAPTER 5:
MY FIRST HOLIDAY

June 24, 2023, marked the first day of my three-week holiday, and I felt almost desperate to pack as much adventure into it as I could. I didn't come all this way to sit still. I came to explore, to stretch into discomfort, and to absorb what Central Australia was willing to show me. One of my first stops was Emily's Gap, outside of Alice Springs—a place I did not yet know would feel like a subtle turning point.

6/24/23 — EMILY GAP

My first time—probably the first of many—visiting Emily Gap. It feels beautiful and serene, almost charged with a peaceful, grounding energy. It may be one of the most beautiful places I have ever witnessed. Magpies swim in the waterhole, and the air hums with nothing but wind and wings. The water blocks access to the ancient artwork, and somehow, that barrier deepens the mystery instead of diminishing it.

Emily Gap, known to the Arrernte people as Anthwerrke (arn-thwer-kuh), is a registered sacred site of immense spiritual significance. It is the primary origin point for the Caterpillar

Dreaming, one of the most important creation stories for the region. Knowing this makes the place feel more alive, more powerful, as if every ridge, every pool, every red rock is vibrating with stories that stretch back thousands of years.

Journal Entry — 6/24/23

I think I found my new meditation place. It's so peaceful here—fresh air, natural sounds, and the weight of history all around me. I want to memorize this place—to carry it with me when everything else feels uncertain.

BEANIE FESTIVAL

During the holiday, I attended the Beanie Festival—an event I heard about in passing but didn't expect to move me the way it did. What began in 1997 as a small local gathering has grown into an event vibrant and layered—a celebration about far more than knitted hats. More than 7,000 beanies filled the space—bright, eccentric, meticulous, each one a small declaration of identity. The beanies created by Indigenous women from communities like Titjikala (titch-ih-kah-lah) and Ampilatwatja (am-pill-AT-wut-cha) were especially powerful—each stitch carrying story, memory, and culture.

But what stayed with me most wasn't the number of beanies or their creativity. It was the feeling in the room. People gathered, talking, laughing, trying on hats. Artists told stories through yarn instead of paint or words. What might seem simple from the outside—a knitted hat—was actually something much deeper.

Each beanie told a unique story. And in a way, so did each of us standing there, carrying pieces of our own journeys. I found myself thinking: If I could create a beanie of my journey, what would it look like? Would it start with shades of grey, to capture being stuck and repetition, slowly changing to brighter colors to mark growth, discovery, and the moments that make me feel fully alive?

For me, the Beanie Festival became a reminder that identity isn't fixed or finished. Like those thousands of beanies, it's what we create over time—thread by thread, experience by experience, shaped by the places we go, the people we meet, and the stories we carry with us on the journey.

Journal Entry — 6/27/23

I went to Yeperenye/Emily and Jessie Gaps today. They sit restfully within the East MacDonnell Ranges. The ranges are woven into the Caterpillar Dreaming story—the story of how Alice Springs came to be.

The gaps contain Aboriginal paintings and are important spiritual sites to Arrernte people. Out of respect, you are not allowed to take photos of the rock art. It is a very magical place, and I will definitely visit again.

I also went to see the dry Todd River. The Todd River usually "runs" through the town of Alice Springs, but most of the time it's dry. There is a local saying: If you see the Todd River flow three times, you will end up staying in Alice Springs forever. I kept hoping to see it flow, as if that might decide something for me.

Journal Entry — 7/1/23

Today is Territory Day, and it's cold and rainy here. On July first, Territorians officially celebrate what they love about this place. The holiday brings mixed feelings—celebration for some, concern for others.

Still, the Northern Territory—and Alice Springs in particular—has introduced me to people whose generosity feels almost undeserved. This place offers stunning desert landscapes, endless opportunities for adventure, and a deep, strong Aboriginal culture.

I ran errands today, bought a scarf and a map of the Larapinta Trail, grabbed groceries, and yes—beer. Things I am learning: After five days of rain, the Todd River remains dry. I was (again) hoping to see it flow, but that might have to wait.

BENEATH THE SOUTHERN SKY

During the holiday, I also had the unique experience of swag camping with my friend Amy. For those unfamiliar, swag camping means heading far into the desert, away from comfort and routine, laying your bedroll directly onto the red earth, and surrendering to whatever the night brings.

It was something I never imagined myself doing—and certainly never imagined enjoying. But I decided to lean into the adventure. I kept asking myself: Why not? What was the worst that could happen?

Amy had quickly become one of the people I trusted most during my time in Australia. From the go, she became my person—the one I laughed with, cried with, and turned to when I needed the kind of hug that steadies your breathing and makes the world feel survivable again. So, when the opportunity came to head out bush together, it felt like the experience that was meant to be shared.

We camped at Rainbow Valley Conservation Reserve, known for its breathtaking sandstone bluffs and cliffs that shift colors at sunrise and sunset. The rocks transform from ochre red to glowing orange and then to purple, creating a natural "rainbow" effect. This land, known as Wurre, holds immense cultural significance for the Southern Arrernte people and is home to ancient rock carvings and paintings.

We kicked off the trip with a stop at The Loco Burrito to fuel up before heading out bush. Once we arrived, setting up camp meant finding a flat patch of red dirt and tossing down our swags. We hiked to Mushroom Rock, a unique sandstone formation shaped— naturally—like a giant mushroom, carved by wind and rain.

As the sun began to set, we found the perfect spot, cooler in tow, filled with beer, cheese, and crackers. I couldn't remember the last time I truly sat still long enough to watch a sunset. And then, almost like my mind was trying to prove me wrong, a memory surfaced—driving home from work one evening back in the U.S., exhausted, mentally replaying the day and already thinking about everything I needed to do when I got home. The sky had been unreal—streaks of orange and pink stretching across the horizon— and for a split second, I actually pulled over. I remember sitting there in my car, engine still running, staring at it. But even then, I don't think I gave it more than a minute or two before I glanced at the clock, convinced I needed to keep going.

And the strangest part? I can't remember what year that was. It felt so long ago, like a different version of me—one who almost paused but didn't quite let herself stay there.

It made me wonder why I waited so long to appreciate beauty so simple and yet so stunning.

Why don't I pause more often to enjoy beautiful moments life offers?

Usually, I rush through my days, counting down to the weekend, only to spend it in bed—scrolling, watching, waiting for a life I claim I want but rarely choose.

Is that really living? Is that how others spend their weekends, too? What's the point of hurrying through life if we never stop to enjoy the beauty along the way?

After sunset, we gathered around the campfire, shared stories, sipped our drinks, and enjoyed being together.

Amy has lived a life shaped by adventure—from living in Canada and traveling around the world to working as a tour guide and now teaching at Larapinta.

She is as real as they come—honest to a fault, deeply grounded, and quietly brave. Amy constantly challenged me to see the world through new lenses—to stretch my empathy, to question my assumptions, and to speak up when something didn't sit right, whether in my own thinking or someone else's. Her presence in my life has grounded me when I felt untethered and empowered me when I felt small.

She was my first true friend in Australia, and I know she will remain one of the constants in my life, no matter where either of us lands. Like Penny, everyone needs an Amy in their life.

That night, I saw the Milky Way with a clarity I didn't know was possible. Amy pointed out the constellations—the Southern Cross (Crux), the Seven Sisters (Pleiades), and the Emu etched in darkness between the stars. She explained how Aboriginal people use the stars to tell time, mark the seasons, and guide decisions about hunting, gathering, and when to allow the land time to rest and renew.

It made me question how we live with the land—not only on it—and how often I moved through places without truly seeing them.

Full honesty: As excited as I was to sleep in a swag, it was far from the most comfortable night of my life. The temperature dropped below freezing, and layered in a coat, hat, and gloves, I had to burrow deep into my swag, curling into myself for warmth. Getting up in the middle of the night to pee? Pure misery.

But when morning came, pride settled over me as steadily as the frost. We woke to a thin blanket of frost covering our swags and the red earth around us. Tiny ice crystals shimmered in the early sunlight—a silent reminder of how cold the night had been.

Back home, I would have never considered camping in below-freezing temperatures, let alone sleeping in a bag laid directly on the ground. But here—on the other side of the world—what I once imagined as pure misery had transformed into moments that filled me with excitement, joy, and an overwhelming sense of being alive.

I made it through the night.

More than that, I felt capable.

This holiday wasn't about seeing new places. It was about learning how to stay still long enough to feel them—and it seems, for the first time, learning how to stay still within myself.

Along the way between the frost and the sunrise, I began to trust myself differently.

Camping at Rainbow Valley.
My favorite flower in the desert: poached-egg daisy

Beanie Festival

Emily and Jessie Gaps: Alice Springs, NT, Australia

CHAPTER 6

AM I ON A DIFFERENT PLANET?

Some days in Australia, the cultural differences felt so extreme I genuinely wondered if I landed on another planet. Everything around me felt unfamiliar—the language, the customs, and especially the creatures. At times, I found myself studying what looked like a harmless little creature and thinking: Is that about to greet me… poison me… or somehow manage to do both?

Australia is home to wildlife found nowhere else on Earth, and I was determined to see as much of it as I could—even if part of me was mildly (okay, sometimes wildly) terrified.

My first encounter with what felt like an alien life form was the processionary caterpillar—better known as the itchy grub. And trust me, the name is not an exaggeration. These are not to be confused with witchetty grubs—large white moth larvae and an important traditional food source for many Aboriginal communities. Witchetty grubs are packed with protein and healthy fats and are often found in the roots of witchetty bushes and river gum trees.

The itchy grubs, on the other hand, should come with a massive warning label: **DO NOT TOUCH.**

They often travel in long, single-file lines, sometimes up to 200 caterpillars, each one following the one in front of it head-to-tail like a slow-moving train of bad decisions. Covered in millions of tiny hairs, they can cause intense skin irritation and severe allergic reactions. Their nests, built high in the treetops, look like giant tangled webs. They may be small, but they are absolutely not messing around.

If itchy grubs made me uncomfortable, snakes made me downright uneasy in my own skin.

Everyone assured me snake bites are rare. What they didn't always mention—at least not gently—is if you do get bitten, your window for help is painfully short. And if you're out bush? Well... you might as well start saying heartfelt well-wishes.

Even though I didn't often see snakes, I was constantly reminded they were everywhere, usually hiding from the heat. I quickly learned to watch where I stepped, where I sat, and especially where I reached without looking first. I did have a couple of unexpected snake encounters, but I'll save those heart-stopping stories for later.

KANGAROO LOVE AT FIRST SIGHT

Then there were the kangaroos.

For every creature that startled me, there was another that softened me.

By far, they are the most iconic, fascinating, and adaptable animals in Australia. And strangely, for the first few weeks I was in the country, I hadn't seen a single one. I imagined kangaroos hopping around everywhere—like squirrels or deer in the woods I know. Instead... nothing.

That all changed the night I visited the Kangaroo Sanctuary.

I had only been in Australia about three weeks when I had my first real kangaroo experience, and it was more than I could have ever imagined. I didn't realize it at the time, but that night would softly reshape the direction of my entire journey.

The sanctuary rescues, rehabilitates, and releases orphaned baby kangaroos back into the wild. Much like deer in the U.S., kangaroos are often hit by cars. If a female kangaroo is found on the roadside, locals are encouraged to check her pouch. If there's a joey inside, the joey is gently placed in a pillowcase and taken to a rescue center like the Kangaroo Sanctuary.

The sanctuary's mission is to educate and inspire people to care for these incredible animals. From the moment I arrived, I could feel the heart behind the work—the care that isn't performative but lived.

The founder, known as Brolga—though his real name is Chris—was given his name by an Aboriginal man. *Brolga* is an Aboriginal word for a tall, long-legged bird, and the name suits him—he's strikingly tall and slender, much like the bird itself.

Some people come for the kangaroos. Others, I think, come just as much to meet Brolga. In certain places, he's something of a celebrity, especially from his time on *Kangaroo Dundee* and his connection to Roger—the famous kangaroo he cared for so deeply, even building a monument in his honor. And yet, none of that seems to matter much to him. He carries it lightly, preferring a quiet, private life centered around caring for his kangaroos and spending time with his wife, Tahnee.

His connection to the kangaroos is truly special to witness.

That night, I fed a kangaroo. I held a tiny joey, wrapped snugly in a pillowcase pouch. And with that, I was done for.

I fell completely in love.

Something turned in me. I didn't want to visit — I wanted to belong. I wanted to become a kangaroo mum.

At first, the sanctuary told me they weren't accepting volunteers. But I wasn't ready to let it go. After several — and I mean several — Facebook messages, I finally got the call. They were willing to train me. (And yes — there's much more to come on that part of the story.)

I used to accept "no" the first time. I told myself it was being respectful, or realistic. But maybe it was also fear — fear of being too much, asking for too much, or hearing no again. This time, something pushed me past that. I kept asking. I let myself want something enough to go after it, even when it felt uncomfortable.

It felt like a door had opened I hadn't known I was allowed to knock on.

I think I'd been waiting for doors to be clearly marked — maybe opened for me. But I'm learning that some of the most meaningful parts of life come from knocking anyway, without knowing what's on the other side.

Life here feels slower, more grounded, more connected — to nature, to people, to the present moment. There's space to notice beauty, follow curiosity, and say yes to the unexpected.

Before this, my life often felt structured, efficient, scheduled. I filled my days, met expectations, checked the boxes. But in doing that, I think I sometimes missed the small, unpredictable moments—the conversations, the faint pauses, the experiences that didn't fit neatly into a plan — the things that might have changed me.

This experience wasn't about feeding a kangaroo. It was about realizing how differently I was living.

And now I can't help but wonder—what would my life in America look like if I carried this version of myself back with me?

RESPECTING THE STORIES WE'RE TOLD

Beyond the wildlife, the cultural language itself often reminded me how far I still had to travel—not physically, but in understanding. Hearing locals casually refer to phrases like "sorry business," "men's business," and "women's business" stirred my curiosity and reminded me how much I still had to learn.

A student once told me his brother was "getting rid of his front tooth." I realized, at that moment, how often I rely on interpretation rather than understanding. I reach for explanations before I've fully listened.

Later, someone suggested it might relate to initiation practices in some Aboriginal communities. Maybe it did; maybe it didn't—but the truth of the moment wasn't really in the explanation. It was in my instinct to make it fit something I already understood.

I didn't get to learn as much about traditional customs as I would've liked. Some communities are understandably wary of outsiders. Certain stories, beliefs, and practices are kept within families, kinship groups, or initiation pathways. This isn't secrecy; it's protection. It's about preserving culture and preventing disrespect or misrepresentation.

Aboriginal cultures in Central Australia hold ancient spiritual beliefs centered around The Dreaming—stories that explain the creation of life, land, and the intricate connections between people, animals, and place. Sacred sites surround Alice Springs — mountains, rock formations, and waterholes that carry strong spiritual meaning and power. Some are open to visitors. Others remain private, accessible only with cultural permission.

Ceremonies held at these sites are significant and often gender specific. Women's business focuses on practices that ensure the health and well-being of the land, community, and future generations. Men's business is reserved for men and is used to teach young males about their roles, responsibilities, and sacred knowledge.

Sorry business refers to the mourning rituals that follow a death. It honors the person who has passed and helps guide their spirit. While it may resemble Western funerals in some ways, the sorry business can last for weeks and affect entire Aboriginal communities.

In some communities, a person's name is not spoken after they pass. Instead, people may use kinship terms like "Aunty" or "Uncle," or a substitute name such as *Kumantjayi* (*koo-MUN-cha-yee*), as a way of showing respect and protecting those who are grieving. This practice may continue for months, years, or in some cases, the person's name may never be used again. Images and recordings of the person may also be avoided during this time. These practices vary between communities, but all reflect a deep care for both the individual and those left behind.

One meaningful way I saw respect for Aboriginal culture expressed was through an Acknowledgement of Country. At the beginning of teacher in-services or public presentations, someone would often say: "I'd like to begin by acknowledging the Traditional Owners of the land on which we meet today and pay my respects to Elders past and present."

Each time I heard it, I felt the weight and the soft-spoken beauty of those words. It was a simple reminder that this land has a story far older than any of us. And being here meant learning not how to live on it, but how to honor it.

Some days, between the itchy grubs, the snakes, the kangaroos, and the cultural language, I truly felt like I was on a different planet.

But slowly, that planet began to feel less foreign—and more like a place that was quietly reshaping who I was becoming.

Kangaroo Sanctuary

Chris Barnes, "Brolga," at the Kangaroo Sanctuary

CHAPTER 7:
HOMESICKNESS: CHANGE IS GOOD?

Even though my first few weeks were filled with adventure and new experiences, there were still moments when homesickness crept in — the kind that settles in your chest and makes you doubt everything.

Had I made a huge mistake?

I traded the known for the unknown — family, friends, routines, comfort — for a life in a place where I knew no one and nothing felt certain. Some days, the excitement carried me. Other days, the doubts were louder.

My mind kept returning to that first night: the fear of being alone in a strange house, the screaming and sirens outside, the shock of my host unexpectedly entering my room. Weeks later, those memories lingered.

Driving around town didn't always help — broken shop windows, buildings boarded up, bars on nearly every window. Most houses were surrounded by tall fences and locked gates. The town carried a tension I hadn't expected, a feeling something could happen at any moment. At times, it felt less like the Australia I imagined and more like a place constantly bracing for impact.

And the truth is, I don't really have a place in the United States to compare it to. Part of that is because I haven't done a lot of traveling, and the places I have gone have looked very different from this. When I chose to vacation or visit somewhere, it was usually all-inclusive resorts—beautiful, easy, predictable. Everything taken care of, everything curated.

And while that might appeal to some, I'm starting to realize that type of travel doesn't let you experience the real culture, the real people, or what daily life actually looks like. It's like seeing a polished version of a place, not the truth of it. It was playing it safe vacation… and if I'm being honest, it mirrored how I was living my life—carefully, comfortably, within boundaries I rarely questioned.

Here, there was no buffer. No curated experience. No neatly packaged version of reality. It was raw, remote, and at times uncomfortable. But now that I'm pushing myself out of my comfort zone, I'm realizing how much there is to learn when you're fully immersed in the good, the hard, and the in-between.

The challenges were visible. Alcohol-related issues. Domestic violence. It wasn't uncommon to see someone passed out on a park bench or slumped outside the grocery store. Youth crime had reached troubling levels, and at times, the town was placed under curfews in an effort to reduce violence and theft.

Strict alcohol restrictions shaped daily life. Alcohol could only be purchased on Thursday, Friday, and Saturday afternoons. Identification was required. Quantities were limited. Some IDs were flagged due to prior offenses, preventing purchases entirely. Police stood at bottle shops, monitoring crowds and stepping in when necessary.

Waiting in long lines, being told how much you could buy and when, felt strange — unsettling. It forced me to reflect not only on the depth of the community's struggles, but on the fragile line between order and chaos... and what might happen if that line disappeared.

But I need to pause here — because this place is so much more than its headlines. If you focus only on the crime, crime is all you'll see. Look closer, and you'll find something entirely different: deep red earth glowing in the afternoon light, an endless desert sky painted with impossible color, wind whispering through gum trees. There's resilience here. Community. A spirit that's hard to explain unless you've breathed in the desert air yourself.

I'm still learning, still trying to understand. But I've realized this: what you choose to focus on shapes what you see. And this place — like any place — is more than its hardest moments.

Journal Entry — 7/16/23

Nothing saps your sense of adventure quite like homesickness. I've felt it lurking beneath the surface for a few days, and it's reared its ugly head. Missing a friend's wedding this weekend is making me ache for home. I never thought I would miss the sound of Brad snoring, but I do.

I find myself picturing the small, ordinary comforts of home. Sitting in my chair with my dogs curled up next to me. The steady pulse of their breathing. The smell of freshly cut grass drifting through an open window — a scent so common at home and completely absent in the desert air. The comfort of my own bed, the familiar weight of the blankets, the way I sink into the mattress without thinking twice. These are the details that make my chest tighten.

There's no shame in feeling homesick. It shows me how deeply I love my family and friends. One thing is for sure: It sucks.

I'm hoping this is a transition stage — that soon Australia will feel more like home. That new sounds and new smells will start to feel like pieces the heart remembers. Nine more weeks until Brad visits, and I'm sure I'll hear my share of snoring then.

FINDING HOME IN THE DEEP END

I remember thinking about how homesickness and change felt a lot like swimming. When you first jump into a cold pool, your instincts tell you to climb out. The shock makes you question why you tried. But if you always got out the second it felt uncomfortable, you'd never learn to swim.

I reminded myself if I could push through the discomfort, over time my body —and perhaps my heart — would adjust. What once felt shocking might someday feel bearable... maybe refreshing.

That's what I was hoping for: If I kept going, kept showing up, and stayed in the discomfort long enough, this strange new place might stop feeling so foreign.

It might start to feel like home.

I already jumped into the ice-cold pool. Of course it was uncomfortable. The shock was part of the process. But if I gave it enough time — if I didn't climb out too soon — I might find ease on the other side.

To get through those early waves of homesickness, I took my friends' advice and started a small list of what I missed most. Of course, I missed my family, friends, and dogs — that goes without saying. But when homesickness hit especially hard, it wasn't always the big changes that undid me.

Sometimes it was the smallest, most ordinary comforts — the parts of life I never realized I'd taken for granted. Writing them down became half comfort, half therapy. A list to smile at later, when Australia began to feel a little more like home.

My List of Things I Miss:

- My chair and watching American TV
- How easy grocery shopping is
  (especially when Brad usually does it)
- Singing to the radio without constantly thinking about driving on the left side
- Not being afraid to sit on a toilet — or walk into a bathroom — wondering what might be in there
- Not needing Google Maps everywhere
- Ice cream
- Dryers
- Spelling the American way
- Hulu
- Picking weeds
  (can't do that here — too many snakes)
- Sleeping with the windows open
  (too scared of creepy crawlies here)

- *My bed — and not imagining things crawling on me at night*
- *Being able to go out after dark and feel safe*
- *Canned pumpkin and Cool Whip*
- *Excedrin Migraine*
- *Hugs*
- *Plastic straws (I can't stand paper ones)*
- *Fireflies*
- *Lucky Charms*
- *Amazon Prime*
- *Erasers, Post-it notes, mechanical pencils, and Papermate felt-tip markers*

Some days, I laughed at this list. Other days, it made me cry.

But writing it down reminded me that missing home didn't mean I was failing. It meant I was human. It meant I loved deeply. And it meant I was brave enough to step far away from the known—and stay, even when it hurt.

Change isn't easy.

CHAPTER 8:
PUMPKIN PIE AND ROSS RIVER

7/17/23 — FIRST DAY, NEW LESSONS

My first day teaching on my own felt exhilarating and unsettling. I started the morning with a Year 3–4 class. Bright faces, eager chatter, and the well-known hum of a classroom stirred emotions in me — a reminder of how much I missed having my own room and my own students.

Later in the day, I covered another teacher's Year 5–6 class, and the energy shifted immediately. The older students were more spirited — sometimes wildly so — and I ended up keeping about five boys in during part of their break to help them refocus.

By the end of the day, I felt a mix of exhaustion and relief. Beneath that exhaustion lingered homesickness. I kept reminding myself to offer myself grace, to breathe, and to trust this feeling would pass. I hadn't come here for comfort. I had come for growth and for something different from the life I knew.

As I drove home that afternoon, red dust rising behind the car, I thought about how each day would hold its own truths — inside and outside the classroom. This was more than teaching. Every challenge, every new moment, was shaping me into someone new.

THE GREAT PUMPKIN HUNT

The next day, I went grocery shopping at the local Woolworths — which was always an adventure. Driving still made me nervous. I was constantly afraid I'd end up on the wrong side of the road. After a long day of work, having to concentrate so fully on driving felt mentally exhausting.

I usually parked far from the store and walked through an area that reminded me of a small American mall. Grocery shopping in Australia often caused stress because I never knew where to find anything. Products had different names, and many items I expected simply didn't exist in the Northern Territory. Yet when they did exist, packaging was so different I would walk past items without recognizing them.

My first memorable shopping experience happened when I tried to buy canned pumpkin.

I asked a store clerk where to find it. She looked at me as if I were speaking another language. I tried to explain, thinking maybe she didn't understand my accent. But the problem wasn't language — it was she had never heard of canned pumpkin.

The situation became a running joke among my coworkers.

I never imagined traveling to Australia, only to discover something as simple as canned pumpkin didn't exist.

When I returned to Penny's house, I told her I couldn't find canned pumpkin, so I wouldn't be able to make pumpkin pie for our camping trip to Ross River.

Penny gave me a look I will never forget — the kind that said she couldn't tell if I was serious or joking.

"Why in the world would you buy pumpkin in a can," she asked, "when you can use fresh pumpkin?"

In America, canned pumpkin is considered the easiest way to make pumpkin pie — as if it were the only proper way.

Penny laughed and told me she would teach me how to cook and puree fresh pumpkin. She was equally shocked when I told her the store didn't carry Cool Whip. When she realized I meant whipped cream, she grinned and said, "You can make that too."

That simple trip to Woolworths reminded me of how everyday habits are rooted in culture. It wasn't about pumpkin or dessert. It was about realizing how far from home I was — and how much I still had to learn.

7/26/23 — FROM PIE TO ROCK MELON

I made two pumpkin pies and brought them to school. The teachers loved them. Most had never tasted pumpkin pie before, so it was fun watching their reactions to their first bite.

In Australia, pumpkin is usually treated as a vegetable rather than a dessert ingredient, so sweet pumpkin was new to many of them.

The pumpkin pie was a hit. Honestly, I couldn't taste much difference between fresh pumpkin and canned pumpkin. When I return to the States, I'll probably stick with the more familiar method.

I also started noticing how many foods here had different names or cultural uses:

- Green peppers are called capsicums
- Muskmelon is called rock melon
- Beets are eaten frequently, even on hamburgers

- Lamb appears in many dishes
- Butter chicken was new to me
- Fairy bread — white bread, butter, and sprinkles
- Pavlova — meringue dessert with fruit and cream
- Meat pies
- Sausage rolls
- Fish and chips
- Vegemite on toast
- Tim Tams
- Anzac biscuits

Food became another language I was learning.

ROSS RIVER CAMPING

On Saturday, we went camping at Ross River.

The drive there was… an experience.

As Penny drove, the road changed from a two-lane highway (locally called *the bitumen*) to a single lane. In time, the bitumen ended entirely, leaving only dirt roads stretching into the outback.

When cars approached from the opposite direction, we moved over — keeping one wheel on the road and one on the dirt shoulder. And we did this at what felt like normal speed, which really meant whatever speed felt comfortable.

The first time a car approached, it felt like a game of chicken. When Penny eased the tires onto the dirt shoulder, I held my breath, convinced this might be the end — for me and for the road.

I shouldn't have doubted her. Penny drove with the confidence of someone who had traveled every imaginable terrain.

At Ross River, Penny stayed in a cabin while I stayed in a small bunkhouse with two sets of bunk beds. Because the weather was cold and no one else was camping, I had the place to myself.

Unfortunately, I developed a severe migraine and became very sick. I spent much of the night vomiting and feeling miserable.

Alone in the bunkhouse, I struggled to stay hydrated, taking tiny sips of water before the nausea rolled back in. The room felt impossibly cold, a cold that settles into your bones, so I wrapped myself in blankets, trying to create a pocket of warmth in a place that felt foreign and far away.

In the darkness, I found myself bargaining with sleep. I prayed I would wake up at home — in my own bed, with my pillows and blankets, with Ozzie curled beside me, the restful flow of his breathing a small, steady reassurance everything was okay. I didn't long for adventure at that moment. I longed for ordinary. For the small, invisible comforts that usually go unnoticed because they are always there.

It struck me how easily we take comfort for granted. Safety is assumed. Familiarity surrounds us so completely we forget it's there. But when you are far from home, truly far, its absence becomes loud. You feel it in the silence, in the darkness, in the way the night stretches longer than it should. Home stops being a place and becomes a feeling you ache for.

That night, comfort felt a world away. And yet, in the middle of that loneliness, kindness found me. Penny took wonderful care of me, checking in and making sure I was okay, a reminder even when you are far from home, you are not completely alone.

By morning, the sickness had loosened its grip. The room didn't feel quite so cold. And I felt an unexpected surge of pride, because I made it through. I survived the night.

Journal Entry — 7/26/23

When I spoke with Brad that week, he shared that he had been feeling depressed, though he said he was starting to feel a bit better.

It made me pause. I realized how much I had been caught up in my own struggles, my own experience here, without fully considering what he might be carrying on his end.

I'm grateful for the way he's supported me in following this path, even when it hasn't been easy. I hope he continues to take care of himself in the ways he needs.

As I think about returning from Australia, I want to hold onto this sense of adventure—to keep choosing a life that feels full and intentional. This experience has stretched me in more ways than I expected. It's taught me to say yes to new experiences, but also to be more mindful—especially with money, and the habits I carry into my everyday life.

Journal Entry — 8/18/23

It's been too long since I last wrote. The past weeks have been a mixture of challenge and growth.

Alice is slowly starting to feel more like a place the heart has known, though it's still far from the comfort and routine of home. I'm learning, almost daily, earning the trust and respect of students here takes time — more than I expected.

Classroom management, a skill I once considered a core strength after more than twenty years of teaching, feels like a constant work in progress. I often find myself frustrated when students talk over my instructions or push against the boundaries I'm trying to set. It's a humbling reminder that experience doesn't guarantee ease in every classroom or context.

At the same time, I do have more freedom in how I teach. I have standards to meet, but there isn't a rigid curriculum I must follow. That freedom allows me to focus on projects, explore creative approaches, and make choices about how to engage the students — which is exciting and also daunting. Every lesson is a balance between structure and experimentation, and each day teaches me a little more about what works here and what doesn't.

I realized quickly that a particular class required a different approach. The traditional "pen to paper" methods weren't reaching them; they needed to move, touch, and build. I began planning activities that allowed them to share their learning through construction rather than solely writing.

After an introductory lesson on electricity, I decided the best way for them to demonstrate their understanding was to create. I challenged them to build their own lighted mini-houses, and the shift in the room was instantaneous. The students were hooked—my most restless student was suddenly focused, his hands busy with wires and tape. In those moments, they weren't only students; they were engineers. They successfully demonstrated simple circuits, and some pushed further, navigating the complexities of parallel and series circuits to make their tiny houses glow.

Still, something about Alice feels like home; it's a home unlike any I've known — one that requires patience, adaptability, and constant reflection. I'm learning to navigate the tension between what I know works, what I hope to achieve, and the unique personalities and dynamics of this classroom.

The last few nights I haven't slept well. My mind keeps thinking about my future.

My wishes for myself one year from today:

- *A job at UNI*
- *A house in Cedar Falls*
- *A small mid-century modern home*
- *Living life fully*
- *Appreciating small things*
- *Being financially mindful*
- *Being proud of myself while caring for my physical, mental, and spiritual health*

Peace. I can do this.

8/20/23 — RAINBOW VALLEY

Homesickness has been close to the surface lately. Part of me wants to retreat from the feelings, to book a flight home and escape the discomfort.

Instead, I went camping with Kirsty — and it was exactly what I needed.

I met Kirsty through Penny and was immediately drawn to her steady presence.

She speaks softly, but when something matters to her — the land, culture, justice — her voice carries depth and clarity. She holds knowledge in a grounded, lived-in way.

I knew I had something to learn from her.

She picked me up in her Red Earth Roaming bus to scout a potential tour route out to Rainbow Valley. My "official" role was to ride along and help assess whether the roads were manageable for future groups, but what I really gained was time — uninterrupted conversation and shared experience.

The drive was rough but breathtaking.

Red earth stretched in every direction, wildflowers bright against the dust, the ranges rising steadily in the distance.

We tossed our swags onto a still patch of dirt away from other campers and carried a cooler to watch the sunset.

Over beers, conversation unfolded effortlessly — music, travel, love, politics, belief systems. Nothing felt rehearsed. Nothing needed to be filled.

After dark, we built a small fire and talked beneath a sky crowded with stars. The desert has a way of stripping away excess. There is no background noise, no distraction —purely wind, space, and the subtle hum of the earth settling.

Camping in the Outback surprised me. I've enjoyed it far more than I anticipated. There is something about swag camping — unzipping your bed to open air, watching constellations stretch endlessly overhead, feeling the first light of sunrise slowly return to the world — that feels grounding.

Simple.

Honest.

Kirsty taught me a lesson without ever formally "teaching." She showed me the best sounds are often the sounds of nature.

That I don't need constant noise — not music, not chatter — to feel full.

Some of the best learning happens in silence. Other lessons come through hard conversations. And sometimes they come while rolling a bottle of wine back and forth between swags.

Her sensitive, adventurous, "we'll figure it out as we go" spirit challenges me.

I tend to want plans. Structure. Purpose neatly mapped out. But occasionally, the best bus adventures are the ones you didn't plan. Sometimes growth happens in unstructured spaces.

Taking in that first morning sunrise — so simple yet so beautiful — felt like a gentle reset.

I feel fortunate for these experiences.

For Kirsty's friendship.

For the reminder I can sit in discomfort and still choose wonder.

I need to keep a positive attitude.

Hold my head up. Keep learning.

Always learning.

Kirsty and Me

Swag Camping

SMALL PIECES FALLING INTO PLACE

Journal Entry — 8/21/23

Two more nights of sleep and I'll be house-sitting for three weeks. After that, I'll have a place of my own. Brad will visit, and for the first time since arriving in Australia, life might feel a little more settled.

Right now, it still feels slightly temporary—like I'm hovering between the life I left behind and the one I'm trying to build. I keep telling myself once I have my own space and Brad is here, life will make more sense. Maybe I'll gain clarity about this journey—how long I'll stay, what I'm meant to learn from it, and what comes next.

Before Australia, I was always waiting for the next thing to make life feel settled—the next break, the next weekend, the next plan. I told myself clarity would come later, once everything lined up the way it was supposed to.

But here, I'm starting to realize that feeling "in between" might not be a problem to fix. It might be a place I'm meant to sit in.

But if I'm honest, the biggest thing weighing on me right now is school.

My Year 5–6 students are testing me in ways I didn't expect. I can't seem to find my rhythm with them, and more importantly, I can't seem to find connection. And without connection, everything else feels like an uphill battle.

Some days I walk out of the classroom completely drained, wondering what I'm doing wrong.

I keep asking myself the same questions over and over.
How do I hold their attention for ninety minutes?
How do I make lessons feel alive instead of forced?
How do I reach them in a way that makes them want to care?

I know connection is the key to respect, and respect is the key to learning. But right now, it feels like I'm standing outside a door I can't figure out how to open.

I had grown used to the systems. Routines. Strategies that worked. I knew how to manage a classroom, how to guide behavior, how to keep lessons moving. Still, when it was hard, there was a sense of control in knowing what to expect. Here, those same methods don't land the same way. And without them, I feel exposed—like I'm seeing my teaching without the safety net I didn't realize I depended on.

There are moments when teaching still feels natural—when I feel confident, capable, proud of the work I do. During those moments, I remember why I chose this profession to begin with.

One of those moments arrived during a lesson on the engineering design process. In a classroom thousands of miles from the nearest snowflake, I shared stories of Iowa winters with students who had only ever known the heat of the Red Centre. I decided to bring that frozen world to life through the Engineering Design Process. Using a fleet of Bee-Bots—small, programmable robots—we set out to solve problems that existed a world away, turning their curiosity into a hands-on adventure in coding and discovery.

I shared photos and videos of a massive Iowa snowstorm, watching their eyes widen as they saw a snowblower for the first time. Most had never seen a snowplow, so we turned it into a research mission: What makes a plow effective? What shape moves the most weight? Working in teams, the students became inventors. They designed and attached custom plows to the front of their Bee-Bots, coding the robots to "plow" through drifts of cotton balls scattered across the floor. We held a contest to see whose design could clear the most "snow" in a single pass. The engagement was electric. In that classroom, thousands of miles from the nearest real snowflake, I felt a profound sense of purpose. I wasn't simply teaching them to code; I was sharing a piece of my home to help them build their own skills. In those moments, I knew I was exactly where I was meant to be.

And there are other days.

Days when I wonder why I traveled halfway around the world to do something that has frustrated me so deeply in recent years.

Teaching in the United States, I sometimes blamed the system, the expectations, the exhaustion. I told myself maybe I needed a change of scenery.
But here I am, in a completely different country, and some of those same feelings are still finding me.
Which makes me wonder... maybe the problem was never the place.

So far, the only conclusion I've reached is kids can be feral in Australia just like they are in America.

And while that observation might be true, it's not nearly enough.

I didn't come this far to give up on understanding them.

At a stage in this challenge, I'm supposed to learn—not strictly about teaching, but about patience, flexibility, and leadership that works without control.

In the past, I relied more on familiarity than I realized. Many of my students came into my classroom already knowing who I was—I taught their siblings or, in some cases, their parents. After more than twenty years in the district, I held a reputation. There was an unspoken understanding of my expectations before I said a word, and that made it easier to build connections and maintain structure.

Here, I'm starting over. No one knows me. There's no history, no built-in trust, no reputation to lean on. Every relationship, every expectation, every bit of respect—I have to build it from the ground up.

And if I'm being honest, it's uncomfortable. It feels like I have to prove myself in ways I haven't had to in a long time. I can't rely on what worked before or who I've been in the past.

But maybe that's the point. Maybe this experience isn't about falling back on what I already know—it's about learning how to build something new, from day one.

If my usual methods aren't working, maybe this is the moment I'm meant to grow beyond them.

Maybe the lesson here isn't for the students.

Maybe it's for me.

Or possibly, for the first time in a long time, I'm being asked to change instead of expecting everything around me to.

Journal Entry — 8/23/23

Tonight is my last night staying at Penny's house, and my heart feels full in that strange way it does when something good is ending.

Tomorrow, I move into a house where I will be house-sitting for two weeks and living on my own for the first time since arriving in Australia. I keep wondering what that will feel like.

Will I enjoy the quiet?
Will I feel lonely?
Will the freedom outweigh the uncertainty?

I suppose I'm about to find out.

I wasn't often alone like this back home. Life was full—family, routines, familiar places, constant noise. Even when I said I wanted space, I'm not sure I ever really gave it to myself.

Here, I don't have the same ways to fill the silence. And I'm starting to wonder if maybe that's the point.

What I do know is leaving Penny's house won't be easy. As time went on, she became more than a generous host who opened her home to me. She became closer to family.

In many ways, she feels like my Australian mum.

She has shared her wisdom, her humor, her stories, and her steady reassurance during moments when I wasn't sure I belonged here. Because of her, Australia has never felt quite as far from home as it could have.

For so long family has always been a constant I could rely on without question.

Here, I'm learning that connection doesn't always come from history. Sometimes it comes from being open enough to let people in, even when they start as strangers.

I know our paths crossed for a reason.

Saying goodbye tomorrow will be hard, but it also feels like the right next step. Living on my own is part of the experience I came here for.

I'm realizing now, so much of my identity was tied to the roles I played—teacher, daughter, partner, friend.

And now, with some of that stripped back, I'm left with a quieter question:

Who am I when it's only me?

A part of me feels nervous. But another part—maybe a bigger part—is starting to believe I can do this.

CHAPTER 10:
A PLACE OF MY OWN

8/28/23 — HOUSE-SITTING

The house was still when I unlocked the door. My suitcase wheels bumped softly across the tile floor as I pulled them inside.

I set my bags down in the middle of the room and stood there for a moment.

It was quiet in a way I'm not used to. No background noise. No one else moving through the space. Just me, the house, and the sound of my own thoughts catching up.

This felt different. Not just a new place—but something shifting underneath it.

Back home, my days filled themselves without much effort. There was always something to do, someone to talk to, somewhere to be. The next step was always waiting.

Here, I have to decide what the day looks like. No one is asking anything of me. No routine is already set.

That feels both freeing and a little unsettling.

The quiet hasn't disappeared the way I thought it might. It lingers. Sometimes it's peaceful. Other times it feels harder to ignore.

But I'm noticing something—I'm not rushing past it in the same way. I'm staying in it a little longer.

I think I'm starting to find my footing here in Alice Springs.

I wouldn't say I love it yet, but something has shifted. The days feel less overwhelming. Instead of counting down how long I'll be here, I'm starting to settle into the rhythm of things—going to school, figuring things out as they come, letting it be what it is.

I'm still unsure, still questioning, but I'm also here in it. Not rushing past it in the same way.

I still don't fully understand why my path led me here.

Of all the places in the world, why this dusty town in the middle of the desert?

I don't have the answer yet.

But I'm starting to feel like I don't need one right away.

Lately, I've been thinking about how I show up—especially at school.
How I build real connections with my students.
How I do the same with the staff around me.
How I move through all of this without assuming I understand things I'm still learning.

I'm realizing not everything needs a quick response. Not everything needs to be filled.

Some things take time.

That's been an adjustment. I'm used to moving quickly—responding, solving, keeping things going.

Here, I'm learning to slow that down. To listen more. To let things unfold without trying to control them right away.

And one thing I can say with certainty: kids are hard everywhere.

That, strangely, brings me a sense of comfort.

Life here feels different in other ways too. Without the constant rush I had at home, the days feel lighter. There's more space—space to think, to notice things I would have missed before.

At first, that space felt uncomfortable. Now, I'm starting to see it differently.

Maybe I don't need to fill every part of my day.

Maybe life doesn't have to move so fast.

If I'm honest about what I want moving forward, it's something simpler.

Less rushing.
More noticing.
More presence in the ordinary parts of the day.

I used to always be looking ahead—planning, preparing, thinking about what was next.

Now, I'm trying to stay where I am.

And for the first time in a while, that feels like enough.

TRANSITION INTO INDEPENDENCE

Before I moved into my donga, life in Alice Springs felt like one long in-between stage. It's common for families here, when they leave for holiday, to find someone they trust to stay in their home — not merely to care for pets, but to make sure the house isn't broken into. The reality is homes left unattended can be vulnerable, sometimes targeted by youth out late at night.

In this case, my house-sitting job came with two dogs and a group of chickens that needed daily care. Each evening, I made my way up the hill to feed them and collect eggs. The light would start to fade, casting long shadows across the dry, dusty ground. The air cooled quickly as the sun dropped, but the stillness of the evening made everything feel sharper, more exposed.

Every step carried a faint tension — the crunch of gravel under my feet, the rustle of dry grass, the constant awareness of what I couldn't see. The thought of snakes hiding near the nests was never far from my mind. My imagination filled in the gaps, convincing me a snake was always out of sight, waiting to strike.

The simple task of reaching into the nesting boxes felt like a test of daringness. I'd pause, take a breath, and remind myself to stay calm — as my heart beat faster than it should have.

And yet, I kept climbing that hill. Night after night.

It wasn't about feeding chickens or collecting eggs — those tasks did, in fact, need to get done. It was about learning to move through fear instead of letting it stop me. About realizing discomfort doesn't always mean danger... even if, in this case, there was a very real possibility it could involve an extremely venomous snake.

Still, it was a reminder not every uneasy feeling is a warning sign — sometimes it means I'm somewhere new, doing something different, stretching in ways I hadn't before.

THE WEIGHT OF SILENCE

It's strange what the mind does when you're alone with your thoughts.

I'm realizing now I didn't often allow myself this rare stillness. My days used to be filled so easily—noise, people, routines that kept everything moving and left little room to sit with my own thoughts.

Here, the silence lingers. And in that silence, everything rises to the surface—louder, clearer, harder to ignore.

Thinking back, the nerves about having my own place were about what the move represented. It wasn't only housing. It was the shift from temporary to rooted — from visitor to resident. That thought filled me with excitement and unease at the same time. Every milestone carries a little fear.

There was comfort in staying where life felt known, predictable.

Now, I'm experiencing the unfamiliar—and while that brings uncertainty, it also brings a feeling of freedom I hadn't experienced before.

Journal Entry — 9/12/23

Tomorrow is the big move into my donga. My body feels like a container of mixed emotions. I'm ready to close the house-sitting chapter, but nervous too. This moment represents something I've been waiting for since arriving — a space that is mine.

I don't want this moment to fall short of what I've imagined.

Journal Entry — 9/14/23

Last night was my first night in the donga. Sleep came in fragments. New sounds. New walls. That restless energy of beginnings.

Once I make this place feel like home, I think rest will come more easily.

I'm used to a different home—the familiar smells when you walk through the door, dogs rushing to greet you like you've been gone forever, although it's only been a few hours. The comfort of sinking into the couch with a favorite blanket, dogs curled up at your feet, everything you need within reach without thinking about it.

Here, none of that exists. Those comforts aren't simply missing—they're on the other side of the world. You can only bring so much with you, and the rest stays behind.

Or perhaps that's part of this experience—learning how to create a sense of home without relying on everything that once made it feel easy.

ALICE CAN DANCE

That night I attended Alice Can Dance, a local event in Alice Springs that brings together dancers from across the Northern Territory to share stories through movement — often highlighting culture, community, and personal expression. Watching those stories unfold was mesmerizing. No photos were allowed, which felt appropriate — maybe memory is stronger than documentation.

It became clear to me how often I would have been reaching for my phone, trying to capture the perfect picture to post on Facebook—adjusting angles, waiting for the right moment, trying to make it look right. Sometimes so focused on capturing it I missed what I was actually trying to hold onto.

Without my phone, I didn't have that option. I watched. I listened. I felt it. And somehow, that made it stay with me in a way a photo never could.

This move feels like life stages:
Living with Penny felt like childhood — safe and protected.
House-sitting felt like college — figuring things out
independently.
The donga feels like adulthood again — independent, proud,
and a little scared.

NIGHTTIME VISITORS

A new place to live comes with new noises, new fears, and new ways your imagination plays tricks on you. Many nights I woke up—or sometimes was already awake—at the sound of a loud scratching noise along the side of my donga, right where my headboard sat. I was convinced a creature was going to come up from under the wall, through the floor, or drop from the ceiling.

I tried to ignore it, pretending it was nothing, but as time went on, I had to say something to the owners, Michael and Heather. They laughed, probably thinking my imagination was running wild, and in truth, they were exactly right. But at two a.m., hearing that noise, I was certain a giant python with sharp teeth was about to attack me and squeeze the life out of me.

Michael and Heather were kind and patient. They suggested it might be a tree branch brushing against the donga in the wind. They trimmed the trees to help. But that night—and the next night—the noise returned.

This time, I decided I would be brave. I grabbed my torch (flashlight, in American language), slipped on my boots, took a long breath, and quietly slipped out the sliding glass door. I rounded the corner of the donga like some sort of nighttime adventurer, ready to confront whatever was lurking, ready to defend myself if necessary.

What I saw instead were three cheeky little rock wallabies, hopping and playing as if they owned the place. My imagined python with giant teeth? Completely nonexistent. I laughed—half relief, half embarrassment—and later told Michael and Heather. They were surprised too; they hadn't realized the wallabies were venturing down to visit.

From that night on, the scratching noise no longer terrified me—it reminded me sometimes, the fears that scare us most are tiny creatures being playful, and occasionally, life gives you a story worth sharing (and laughing about) the next morning.

My Donga

9/17/23 — DESERT MOB FESTIVAL

I went to Ormiston Gorge in the West MacDonnell National Park with Kirsty and Penny, a spectacular, dramatic landscape defined by towering red quartzite cliffs, ghost gum trees–lined sandy banks, and a near-permanent, sunken waterhole that seemed to hold the reflection of the sky itself. The gorge felt alive in a way that made the world outside fade.

While I was there, I listened to the Central Australian Aboriginal Women's Choir — a group of local Indigenous women whose songs carry language, history, and faith passed down through generations. Their voices were ancient, powerful, and strongly connected to the land, as if the songs had risen straight from the cliffs and red dirt around me. The music seemed to carry the stories of the land itself, a reminder this place has held life, memory, and meaning far longer than I could ever comprehend.

It was one of those rare days that feel almost unreal while they are happening — a day you know will stay with you long after you leave.

Moments like that don't come from rushing or planning every detail. They come from being present enough to notice where you are.

By the next morning, anticipation returned. Brad was on his way.

CHAPTER 11:

BRAD ENTERS THE OUTBACK

Journal Entry — 9/18/23

Today is the day! Brad arrives at 12:15.

I'm excited — almost painfully excited — but nervous too. I already dread the loneliness that will come after he leaves. I know emptiness well.

For now, I am reminding myself to stay present. To enjoy what is happening instead of mourning what will at some point end.

The days that followed were filled with laughter, small adventures, and comfort.

At the mall, police randomly patted Brad down for weapons. He handled it calmly.

Later, we discovered a large creature on my veranda.

Brad yelled, "Becky — come here, quick!"

I refused to go outside.

I took a photo and sent it to the school secretary:
What is this thing on my veranda?

She responded laughing — it was a perentie lizard. Apparently, a baby. The idea of a full-grown one still terrifies me. Australia keeps reminding me how wild and alive it is.

STANLEY CHASM

I waited to visit Stanley Chasm until Brad was here. I heard from several people it was breathtaking and absolutely a must-see.

The truth is, I didn't know what a chasm was when I heard the word. A steep gorge split into the earth, rock walls rising on either side as if the land had cracked open. That was the definition. But definitions don't prepare you for the Outback.

I read around noon the sun drops directly between the towering walls and ignites the sandstone. For a short window each day, the cliffs glow — the reds intensify, the oranges burn bright, and the rock seems to hold the light inside itself.

So, we arrived early and slowly followed the path toward the chasm.

The air felt still, and the farther we walked, the calmer everything became. Our footsteps softened. The stillness made us aware of every step, every small movement around us — a bird's shadow gliding across the sand, a lizard slipping between stones, the transforming patterns of light against the rock.

Stanley Chasm is a sacred place for the Arrernte people who have lived on this land for thousands of years. Even without fully understanding its meaning, you can feel it holds knowledge older than explanation. The space feels still, but not empty. It feels watched over.

We reached the base of the chasm nearly an hour before noon. The walls rose steeply around us, narrow at the bottom and stretching so high you had to tilt your head back to see the thin strip of sky above.

Then the sun began to shift.

Slowly, a column of light dropped between the towering walls. Within moments, the sandstone transformed. The red deepened past red. The orange flared like fire. The cliffs didn't look lit from the outside — they looked alive, glowing from a place buried within.

I took a picture with my phone. When I looked at the image later, it almost appeared as though the earth itself was opening — gently, like a hand offering comfort.

I was only three months into my time in Australia. On the outside I was building a life in the Outback — learning my job, finding my way around town, learning to drive on the opposite side of the road, adjusting to the pulse of a place completely different from home.

But inside, I was holding my breath.

There's a muted disorientation that comes with leaving everything trusted behind. Including when the decision is yours, part of you wonders if you've stepped too far away from the life you once knew.

Standing there in that narrow canyon of light, a different thought came to me. If I hadn't taken that leap, I never would have seen this place. I never would have felt this moment.

Maybe it was time to stop holding my breath.

It was a chance to breathe in the beauty around me and allow the experience to change me. It wasn't about playing it safe or staying tucked inside the comfort of my donga or the routine of my classroom. It was about saying yes to the opportunities in front of me and taking in as much as I could while I was here.

The desert, with all its space and silence, had been discreetly working on me.

It had created a space I didn't know I needed — a space wide enough to rediscover the curiosity and sense of adventure I felt when I was younger. Before stress, before pressure to keep up with everything life seems to demand. Before the constant pull to fit in or keep up.

Out here, no one knew me.

No one had expectations or assumptions about who I was supposed to be.

I was simply free to be myself.

Free to feel excited again.
Free to wander.
Free to explore the land stretching out in front of me.

And maybe that was the greatest gift the desert was giving me — not answers, but space.

Space to wander.
Space to notice.
Space to be myself.

Stanley Chasm

CHAPTER 12

TRAVEL SUMMARY - RED CENTRE + TOP END

"In the Northern Territory, the land does not merely surround you — it watches you." — a saying I heard often while living in the NT

(AUTHOR UNKNOWN)

We traveled through the Red Centre and Top End, moving through landscapes that felt like continuous motion.

DIMPLES, DUST, AND THE DREAMING

We loaded up Dimples — my trusty car, road-worn and reliable, the best travel companion — and pointed her nose toward a landscape so ancient it makes the rest of the world feel young. The plan was simple in the way all great adventures are: Get out there, be present, and let the Red Centre do what it does.

The silence of the desert was different. For months, the Outback had been a conversation I was having with myself. Now, with Brad in the passenger seat, I felt a nervous hum of electricity. I wasn't only showing him a tourist destination; I was showing him the place that had reshaped me. I found myself watching him out of the corner of my eye, silently rooting for the desert to work its magic on him the way it had on me. I wanted him to see what I saw, to feel the pull of the red earth, and maybe—just maybe—to see a future for us that lasted longer than his return ticket. The Outback can be an isolating, beautiful beast, but with Brad there, the edges felt softer. I wasn't a solitary woman navigating the wild anymore; I had a witness.

DESERT SPRINGS: WHERE THE JOURNEY BEGINS IN STYLE

Our first stop was the Desert Springs Hotel, and beautiful doesn't begin to cover it. Set against the vast ochre palette of the outback, it felt like a jewel dropped in the middle of nowhere — which is, of course, exactly what it was.

That first evening was nothing short of magical. We were taken out to dine as the sun made its slow, spectacular descent behind Uluru. The great monolith changes color as the light shifts, cycling through shades of amber, blood orange, violet, and finally a bold silhouette black as darkness claims the desert. We sat with drinks in hand, the warm air carrying feelings that can only be described as the breath of the ancient world.

And then the didgeridoo started playing.

The sound it produces is unlike anything else: a low, circular, droning vibration seems to travel through the ground as much as the air. Between that sound and the view, it was one of those moments where you stop talking because anything you say would probably ruin it.

After dinner, our guide turned our eyes upward to the sky, and the real show began. Out here, far from the light pollution that robs city people of the universe, the Milky Way arches overhead like a road map to eternity.

Our guide started explaining how the night sky has meaning beyond stars — stories, navigation, connection — teachings that have been passed down for thousands of years. I didn't catch all of it, but I understood enough to realize this wasn't about looking up. It was about understanding where you are in a much bigger picture. For months, I'd been navigating the red dust on my own, proving my independence. But standing there with Brad, I realized as much as I loved the solitude, the "bigger picture" was much warmer when shared. I wanted him to feel that connection to this life.

We ended the evening walking through the Field of Lights. I don't know how to fully describe it. It felt like walking into a dream. Over fifty thousand frosted-glass stems rise from the earth like luminous wildflowers, pulsing and breathing through gradients of color: stark magenta, soft gold, ocean blue, ghostly white.

I remember walking slowly through it, not really saying much, hearing the crunch of the dirt under my feet. Uluru was out there in the distance, mostly dark now, watching over everything. There are a reason people travel from every corner of the earth to stand here.

KINGS CANYON: ANCIENT WALLS AND OPEN SKY

The next morning, I started feeling sick, and the flies at Kings Canyon tested my patience. We laughed through it anyway, wearing fly nets like explorers. Even beauty has discomfort.

Instead of the rim walk, we visited Kathleen Springs. The Rainbow Serpent story made the day feel deeply meaningful.

Kathleen Springs is more than a peaceful waterhole — it holds substantial meaning. It is believed to be protected by the Rainbow Serpent, a powerful ancestral being connected to water, life, and creation.

The serpent is said to keep the spring alive, guarding it and ensuring the water continues to flow. There is a soft-spoken understanding that if the serpent were ever disturbed or chose to leave, the waterhole itself could disappear.

Because of this, the Luritja people have long treated the area with great respect. They would camp at a distance and avoid entering the water, honoring the presence of a spirit far greater than themselves.

That respect still carries through today. Swimming at Kathleen Springs isn't allowed, and the area is meant to be experienced gently— not as a place of beauty, but as a place with meaning, history, and a story that continues long before and beyond any visitor who passes through.

I surprised Brad with a helicopter ride over Kings Canyon. I went into the helicopter ride fully expecting to be nervous. Maybe even scared.

That lasted about five seconds.

As soon as we lifted off, everything opened up. I got the front seat, right next to the pilot, with nothing but glass in front of me. You could see straight down, straight out —endless land. Looking down at the red landscape, the truth found me, this is what living feels like — being fully present, not distracted by constant noise.

The pilot was talking, explaining details about the land... but honestly, I barely heard him. I was too busy looking.

There was no fear. Not a flicker. Purely the clean, uncomplicated joy of being

airborne over the beautiful land. I thought about how much I had grown and smiled to myself. Not so long ago, this would have been unthinkable. Now it was just Tuesday.

KARRKE: LEARNING TO LISTEN

If the helicopter showed me Kings Canyon from above, the Karrke Aboriginal Cultural Experience brought me down into the heart of it. Karrke is an Aboriginal-owned tour outside Watarrka National Park, and its name comes from the word for the western bowerbird — the bird collects little treasures to build something meaningful. That felt fitting, because that's exactly what this place does. It gathers stories and knowledge and passes them on.

The tour is an unhurried, one-hour walk and talk through shaded outdoor areas, and it's one of the most genuinely enriching tours I have done anywhere. We learned about bush tucker — the seasonal foods gathered from the land: edible seeds, grass seeds, and yes, the witchetty grub, plump and slightly nutty and absolutely not as alarming as its reputation suggests.

We learned about bush medicine too, the plants used for healing, for spiritual practices, for protection against the insects and heat of the desert.

We examined wooden artifacts — spears balanced for throwing, boomerangs shaped for specific purposes, not all of which return as it turns out, only certain types are designed to do so.

They demonstrated jewelry making as well, using organic tree seeds burned with traditional branding techniques into intricate patterns, each one carrying its own meaning.

KINGS CREEK STATION: BRAD AND THE TOWEL BARRICADE

Our accommodation for the Kings Canyon leg of the journey was Kings Creek Station, and I can tell you with complete sincerity it was more my vibe.

Kings Creek Station is a working cattle and camel station and operates as one of the most authentic Outback accommodations in the country, still running cattle and exporting camels while welcoming travelers with the rare hospitality only remote country people seem to have perfected.

We stayed in the bush tents — a step up from a swag on the ground, but not by a margin that would satisfy anyone seeking spa amenities. Set against the magnificent backdrop of the George Gill Range, the tents are simple structures with two single beds, power, lighting, and air conditioning. Shared toilet and shower facilities are nearby. A camp kitchen is a fire pit.

It was perfect.

For me, at least.

Brad had a different relationship with the accommodation. Brad isn't one who sleeps easily with the knowledge that the Outback is just on the other side of a canvas wall, and canvas walls aren't, technically speaking, sealed environments. As I was settling into the particular contentment that comes from being close to the earth with the stars overhead, Brad was conducting a thorough structural assessment of the tent's perimeter.

He gathered the spare towels. He folded them and placed them along the gap at the bottom of the door to ensure nothing — no spider, no centipede, no snake, no hypothetical creature of the outback night — would find its way into our sleeping quarters uninvited.

I found this quietly amusing.

And I had to laugh... softly, of course.

Because the truth is, I swag camped. I slept straight on the ground under the open sky — no tent, no barrier, no towels, and definitely no plan for what might wander by in the middle of the night.

That's how it's done out here.

So, standing there watching him "fortify" the tent with hotel towels, I had this moment when it hit me... not that he was being over the top — but I changed. I looked at his city-clean Nike shoes and his cautious movements, then down at my boots, permanently stained red and resting easy on the dirt floor.

Not long ago, I probably would've been doing the same thing. Maybe also adding extra towels to be safe.

I became the person who found it funny instead of necessary. I realized while I wanted him to love this place, I had already found a version of myself here who didn't need the towels anymore. I was finally comfortable in the wild, yet my piece of "home" was still triple-checking the gaps in the canvas door.

ULURU: THE ROCK THAT HOLDS EVERYTHING

Nothing prepares you for Uluru. Not the photographs, not the documentaries, not the people who've been and come back trying to describe it. The moment it rises from the flat desert floor, you understand why words have always failed it. Ancient, enormous, and somehow personal, as though it has been waiting for you specifically and has all the time in the world.

Standing 348 meters above the plain and extending kilometers below the surface, what you're seeing is only the tip of something vast. The rock is 550 million years old, its iron minerals slowly oxidizing into that famous red-orange glow. But the geological story, as extraordinary as it is, is the lesser one.

Uluru is the sacred home of the Anangu people, who have lived here for more than 30,000 years. To them, it isn't a landmark or a wonder of nature — it's a living part of the Tjukurpa, the Dreaming, the law and story that holds together all relationships between people, land, animals, and time. Not a creation story in the way we typically understand one, but something ongoing — past, present, and future existing all at once. The caves, the waterholes, the overhangs — each one carries specific spiritual meaning and obligation. Once you understand that, the request not to photograph certain areas feels less like a restriction and more like the bare minimum of respect.

The rock's surfaces change constantly as you walk around the base: smooth in one place, roughly fractured in another, stained dark where ancient waterfalls once ran. I walked slowly. I let myself be still. When I completed the circuit, I wasn't sure I could explain what I felt, but I knew I'd been in a corner of the world that mattered in a way most places simply don't.

I let it be exactly what it was.

THE ROAD BACK TO ALICE

As all journeys must, this one turned toward home. Dimples pointed north and east, back toward Alice Springs. The drive back demanded the same alert attention as the drive out. This isn't a road where your mind can wander far from the task at hand. Wild brumbies — feral horses appear suddenly at the roadside, along with feral camels, who lumber across the road with the confidence of creatures who know they are larger than anything they are likely to meet. Kangaroos, as always, show up without warning. When I tapped the brakes, I could see Brad scanning the scrub with the intensity of a man expecting an ambush. To me, it was only the local traffic; to him, it was a high-stakes game of survival.

You drive with your eyes wide open, and the country rewards that attention. Every kilometer of the road back was a painting: the spinifex catching the afternoon light, the mulga trees casting their sparse shadows, the desert oaks that stand in the creek beds with their drooping, sigh-like branches. The red earth. Always the red earth, impossibly vivid, staining everything it touches — your shoes, your wheels, the hem of your jeans, the edges of your memory.

I drove and thought about everything I had seen and done and felt over these days. About the Field of Lights blooming in the desert dark. About the stars and the dark constellations and the stories that hold the sky together. About Brad and his towel barricade. About the sound of the didgeridoo at sunset and the way Uluru changes color like something breathing. About the front seat of a helicopter and the complete, uncomplicated absence of fear.

The Red Centre gives you a lot to carry back with you. I was grateful for every bit of the weight and even more grateful that for a few hundred kilometers, I didn't have to carry it alone.

Dimples drove us home.

DARWIN, THE ADELAIDE RIVER, & LITCHFIELD NATIONAL PARK: WHERE THE WILD THINGS RULE

Some places don't feel tamed. You know right away you're not in charge. Darwin felt like that—a hot city on the edge of something bigger and wilder. It didn't feel like arriving. It felt like stepping into the unknown.

We heard the warnings. Lots of them. The Northern Territory is home to something like 100,000 saltwater crocodiles, which is honestly hard to wrap your head around. It's one thing to read that number or see a sign and another thing entirely to realize you're standing in a place where they actually live.

And realization hit quickly — on the Adelaide River, before I had fully woken up or had a proper cup of coffee.

The Adelaide River sits about an hour outside of Darwin along the Stuart Highway, a long, flat stretch of road that feels like it could go on forever. We booked one of the jumping crocodile tours and pulled up to the boat ramp as the heat was starting to settle in. By nine a.m., it already felt like someone had wrapped me in a warm, wet towel I couldn't take off.

The river itself didn't look like much at first — only muddy water winding through wide-open land — but knowing what lived in it changed everything. Saltwater crocodiles have been here for millions of years. They haven't adapted to this environment... They are the environment. And we were about to go floating right through the middle of it.

The boat was a wide, flat pontoon packed with people trying to look calm and brave. Before we left the bank, the guide started talking about the "regulars" — crocodiles they knew by name. Like this was a neighborhood and not a river full of predators. There was one missing a limb; another known as the big one, apparently large enough to make every other crocodile think twice. I nodded along like this was all normal information to receive before getting on a boat.

Then we pulled out onto the river.

At a certain point, the guide leaned over the side with a piece of meat on a pole, and within seconds, the water exploded. That's the only way to describe it. One minute it was calm, and the next, this massive, armored body launched straight out of the water. It didn't feel real — it felt like watching something from another period.

What got me wasn't how big they were — it was how fast. One second nothing, the next second pure power. I kept thinking, *We are sitting in a floating platform in the middle of their home*, and by the look on Brad's face, he was thinking the exact same thing, probably wondering if "towel barricades" worked against twelve-foot apex predators.

The tour lasted about an hour and a half, drifting along while crocodile after crocodile appeared out of nowhere. By the end, I was equal parts amazed and slightly on edge, like my brain was still trying to process what I had seen.

THE MAGNETIC TERMITE MOUNDS: ARCHITECTURE OF THE ANCIENTS

On the drive south from Darwin, before turning toward Litchfield, we made a stop I could almost have missed if I hadn't been paying attention. Off the Stuart Highway, the land opened up into this wide, flat grassy plain—and suddenly, there they were.

Hundreds of them.

Dark, thin shapes rising out of the ground, all standing in the same direction like they had been placed there on purpose. It stopped me in mid-sentence. I remember standing there for a minute, trying to make sense of what I was looking at.

These were the magnetic termite mounds, and somehow, tiny creatures had built all of it. Each mound was carefully lined up north to south, like they had their own built-in compass. I later learned it helps control the temperature inside, protecting them from the intense heat.

Some mounds were taller than me, solid and weathered, almost like they had been there forever. And yet, you couldn't see a single termite. Not one. It felt strange, standing there surrounded by all that work and not seeing the workers.

It made me think about how much can exist beneath the surface—how something so small, almost invisible, can build something so lasting. No blueprints. No instructions. Strictly instinct and time. Brad, however, did not share my enthusiasm. For him, the mounds were just high-rise apartments for things that crawl. Brad was ready to be in a world where the bugs didn't build monuments.

Off to the side were the cathedral termite mounds, completely different—tall, uneven, and wild-looking, like melted towers reaching up toward the sky. They felt chaotic compared to the serene order of the magnetic mounds. Side by side, it was like seeing two completely different personalities written into the land. I pointed out the differences to Brad, who was now standing with his hands deep in his pockets, looking like someone who had reached his absolute limit on educational nature stops.

LITCHFIELD NATIONAL PARK

Litchfield National Park sits about 130 kilometers south of Darwin, but it felt like we were driving into a completely different world. The long, flat stretch of highway slowly gave way to a road more layered, more alive. The land started to rise, cliffs appearing in the distance, and the vegetation turned to thick, green pockets of forest tucked into low areas, open stretches of dry woodland, and swampy patches that looked like they belonged in another climate entirely.

We followed the main road through the park, stopping at the well-known spots— Buley Rockhole first, Florence Falls, and at last, Wangi Falls. Each spot felt different, like pieces of the same story unfolding one stop at a time.

BULEY ROCKHOLE: THE FIRST PLUNGE

Buley Rockhole was our first stop, and I wasn't quite prepared for how beautiful it would be. A short walk brought us down to a series of natural pools where clear water spilled over smooth rock ledges, creating these little cascading sections that looked almost too perfect to be real.

People were already there — kids jumping in and immediately screaming from the cold, adults easing themselves in a little more cautiously, settling into that look of pure relief once their bodies adjusted.

Swimming in Buley Rockhole, I was acutely aware of a concern that would become a recurring sensation throughout the day: the specific pleasure of cool, clean, running water in an intensely hot landscape, and — beneath it, never entirely absent — a small, persistent awareness of where we were.

Crocodile country.

The signs at every waterhole were explicit: These waterholes are regularly monitored by park rangers. If a crocodile is sighted, the area will be closed immediately. Swimming is only permitted when the signs indicate it is safe to do so. Brad, however, did not find "regularly monitored" to be a particularly comforting phrase. To him, it sounded like a suggestion rather than a guarantee. He stood on the edge for a long time, watching a child splash around. If the kid stayed in one piece, maybe the water was safe.

I assumed the system worked. The Northern Territory Parks and Wildlife service have maintained a consistent monitoring program at Litchfield's swimming holes for decades. Rangers check these waterholes consistently using a combination of foot patrols and spotlighting. Any freshwater crocodile is noted and monitored. Any saltwater crocodile — vastly more dangerous — triggers an immediate closure. The swimming holes have an excellent safety record precisely because the monitoring is taken seriously.

Brad eventually joined me in the water, but "relaxing" wasn't exactly the word I'd use to describe his swimming style. He stayed in the shallowest possible section, moving with a stiff, upright posture, suggesting he wanted as little of his body submerged as possible. Every time a leaf brushed against his leg, he practically levitated out of the water.

Emotionally, though, you're swimming in the Northern Territory. The knowledge that, in an unassuming place downstream — perhaps not far — the rivers widen and the big ones come in from the coast doesn't entirely leave you. It sits whispering in the back of the mind, lending a particular intensity to the experience. The water feels colder than it is, and your senses are dialed up a notch! It was a lesson in Territory life: beauty and danger live in the same pool, and sometimes, the best way to enjoy the view is to have a partner who is willing to be the designated croc-watcher while you soak it all in.

FLORENCE FALLS: FALLING INTO ANOTHER WORLD

After Buley Rockhole, we kept driving, not really knowing how anything could top what we had seen. And then we got to Florence Falls.

There are two ways to get down — a long walking track or a steep set of stairs carved right into the cliff. We took the stairs. At the time, it felt like a good idea. About halfway down, I started questioning that decision... and also realizing I'd sooner or later have to come back up.

But then we reached the bottom, none of that mattered anymore.

You round that last corner, and it expands in front of you.

Two streams of water fell side by side over the rocks, straight down into this deep, clear pool surrounded by thick green trees. The air was cooler near the water, the mist drifting out enough to take the edge off the heat. Everything around it felt alive — the sound of the falls, the movement of the trees, flashes of birds cutting through the air.

The water was deep and cold, and swimming out toward the falls felt a little surreal — like the closer you got, the more everything else faded out. The noise of the water took over, loud and steady, until it was the only thing you could hear.

I remember floating there for a minute, looking up, trying to take it all in.

THE PERENTIE: ROYALTY IN REPTILE FORM

In transit between Florence Falls and Wangi Falls, along one of those shaded paths that wind through the trees, we turned a corner, and there he was.

At first, I didn't process what I was looking at. And it hit me.

This lizard was huge.

It was a perentie — the largest lizard in Australia — and apparently, no one had ever told him to be afraid of humans.

He kept walking. Slow. Steady. Completely unbothered.

His tongue flicked in and out like he was casually tasting the air, and for a brief second, he glanced in our direction with one eye — not scared, not curious... aware. Like we were the ones who had wandered into *his* space.

Which, to be fair, we had.

He didn't rush. Didn't change direction. Didn't hesitate. Solely continued across the path like he had somewhere to be, and we weren't part of the plan. His claws made a subtle clicking sound on the rock, his long tail dragging behind him like he owned the land.

And honestly… he more or less did.

We stood there in silence watching him disappear into the brush, and it felt like one of those moments you don't really need to talk about. You let it sink in. I looked at Brad and saw that look again—the one that said he was currently reconsidering every outdoor activity we had planned for the rest of the day.

WANGI FALLS: THE CROWN OF LITCHFIELD

Wangi — the name comes from the local Koongurrukun language, and there is some debate about its precise meaning, though it is often translated as referring to a spring or water source — is in every way the showpiece of the park.

By the time we reached Wangi Falls, I thought I carried a pretty good idea of what to expect.

I was wrong.

The falls here drop approximately eighty meters from the plateau rim in two large cascades

over a broad sandstone face, filling a large swimming lagoon at their base that is substantially bigger than the plunge pools at Florence and Buley.

There was a sign at the entrance showing the latest crocodile check. No sightings. Open for swimming.

I read it. I believed it.

And so, we swam. In the shadow of the falls, with eighty meters of white-water crashing down the rock face in front of us and the rainforest rising on all sides, we swam in what is probably the finest natural swimming hole I have ever encountered. The water was cool without being cold, silky from the minerals and so clear near the falls you could see every detail of the sandy bottom.

We drove back to Darwin as the sun went down over the Timor Sea, the sky doing extraordinary displays in shades of orange and violet, the floodplains turning gold on either side of the highway. Out there in the darkening river systems, the big crocodiles were settling back into the water after the day's warmth. The termites were doing whatever termites do in the hours we cannot see. The perentie had gone wherever perenties go.

We were leaving in the morning, heading back to Alice, and I was already looking for reasons to come back.

Crocodile Tour

Brad and me at Uluru

Uluru

Culture Experience - Kings Canyon

Termite Mound in Darwin

10/4/23 — WHEN THE QUIET RETURNS

Our last full day in Darwin was spent at the Mindi Beach Casino Resort. The ocean stretched out in front of us, calm and endless, but my mind felt anything but calm. It was crowded with thoughts I couldn't quite sort through.

As Brad's time here came to an end, the sadness settled in quietly. I knew this goodbye was coming from the moment he arrived, but that didn't make it any easier. The closer it got, the more I wondered what the days would feel like after he left—how I would settle back into this life I was building without him beside me.

My heart actually ached—a sharp, persistent throb. I found myself looking at him and desperately trying to find a way to make him stay. I played through every scenario in my head, trying to piece together a life where he didn't have to get on that plane.

But as I watched him scan the horizon—likely still looking for crocodiles or centipedes—the truth settled in.

Down deep, I knew this wasn't his dream. It was mine.

The things that brought me happiness—the staining red dust, the isolation of the donga, the wild unpredictability of the critters, and the raw vulnerability of swag camping—weren't the things that brought him joy. He had embraced it all for me, he had been a good sport through the flies and the heat, but Brad would never want to live here. He would never be truly happy in a place that required towel-barricaded doors simply to get a night's sleep. It brought *me* happiness, but for him, it was a world he was merely visiting.

That was the hardest part of saying goodbye. It wasn't purely about missing him in the weeks to come; it was the realization by choosing the Outback, I was choosing a path that diverged from his. I knew eventually I would have to say goodbye to the place

I love to be with the person I love. I was standing between two lives, and both required a sacrifice.

To keep from slipping into emptiness, I gave myself a goal to hold onto: volunteering at the Kangaroo Sanctuary, helping rescue and raise baby joeys. It felt like a lifeline for my future self—meaningful waiting for me when the loneliness returned.

Goodbyes have a way of showing you what really matters. If they were easy, it would probably mean something important was missing. These weeks together meant more than I can fully put into words. Sharing this with Brad—letting him see the life I've been creating here—grounded me in a way I didn't expect.

But now it was ending, and it was time for me to come back to the purpose that drew me here from the start. I had not crossed oceans and time zones — uprooted myself from everything familiar — simply to return unchanged, a mirror image of the woman who had stepped off that plane with uncertainty pooled in her chest. I wanted to emerge with a courage I hadn't yet earned and to carry forward, into every ordinary day, a gratitude for the extraordinary gift of being alive to live it.

I promised myself I wouldn't leave Australia without stepping fully into whatever this experience was meant to teach me. To excavate my confidence from wherever it had buried itself and to rediscover a sense of purpose deeper than the life I was merely moving through.

When Brad goes home the space left behind would be mine again. That's where the real work begins—not the kind you do at a job, but the kind that asks you to sit with discomfort, face your fears, and trust that growth happens there.

Looking ahead, I feel a quiet determination. I want to say yes to new experiences. I want to keep learning the small bits of life that make Alice feel like home—practicing the ukulele, noticing the animals around my donga.

But more than anything, I want to keep building connections—with my students, with the people around me, and with this life I am learning how to live.

This journey was never meant to be easy.

It was meant to change me.

And I can feel it already has.

RED EARTH, OPEN SKY

A NIGHT IN TREPHINA GORGE

Trephina Gorge sits about eighty-five kilometers outside Alice Springs, tucked into the East MacDonnell Ranges.

This land has been part of the Eastern Arrernte people's story for thousands of years, connected to the Wallaby Dreaming Trail and holding meaning that goes far beyond what you can see.

The gorge itself is rugged and wide — tall rock walls, sandy creek beds, and trees growing in areas that don't seem possible. Birds move through the area, and if you're lucky, you might catch a glimpse of a rock wallaby moving along the cliffs.

You don't need much more than that.

THE DRIVE OUT

Kirsty picked me up in her ute, and we headed out toward Trephina, with Amy meeting us there later. The drive east of Alice felt open and calm, the red dirt stretching out and the ranges rolling alongside us.

We stopped for a sight you cannot in good conscience drive past: the largest ghost gum in Central Australia. It stands alone on a saltbush flat within the park, a single white-barked tree commanding the plain around it with understated authority. There's a deep stillness to a tree that has simply endured — through drought and flood and the slow grinding of centuries — while everything around it changed.

When we reached the campsite, it became clear almost immediately we were going to need to move. The site we'd landed on put us too close to other campers — and for Kirsty, that simply won't do. She is a woman who comes to the desert for the desert: for the silence, the space, the utter absence of other human noise. I respect this entirely.

We relocated, spreading our swags out on the red earth at a distance that satisfied the need for proper solitude.

Amy arrived, and the three of us decided to take one of the walking trails to the top of the ridge. It was described as one of the easier trails. I want to be unmistakably clear about this: Easy is not a word I would choose. My heart was doing things hearts are not meant to do. My legs had opinions. The ground was uneven and unforgiving. And yet, I kept going, because I could feel what was waiting at the top before I arrived. The air grows bigger. The world becomes quieter. I sensed the scale of what I was climbing toward. And then I was there. The only word that came was open.

I felt like I was standing on top of the entire world. The ranges rolled away in every direction, the red earth spread below laid out to be witnessed, and the sky — enormous, magnificent Central Australian sky — sat above all of it like a promise.

I tried to photograph it, of course. We all did. But the camera doesn't catch what your hole body is feeling in a moment like that — the clean air moving through you, the particular quality of silence that isn't actually silence at all, but rather everything humming at a frequency your ordinary life doesn't tune into. There are moments that must live in memory, and this is one of them. Not in a folder on your phone, but in a place deeper — in the calm spaces you return o during meditation, in the half-lit territory of dreams, in those private moments when ou need to remember beauty on this scale is real, and you have touched it.

We sat there at the edge of those cliffs and breathed. I breathed the way you breathe when you're trying to hold on — as though enough of the clean desert air, pulled inward enough, would deposit the beauty in the marrow of my bones permanently.

The descent was, I'm grateful to report, significantly more forgiving than the climb. We made our way back down through the fading light, the ranges shifting color around us as the sun lowered.

THE UNINVITED GUEST AT THE PARTY

Our swags were laid out on the red earth, a small fire had been coaxed into being, and we had food and conversation and stars that only happen when there's no city light for hundreds of kilometers in any direction.

And then, out there in the near distance, music. Not the rustle of nocturnal animals, not the low percussion of the desert at rest — but music, loud and thumping, spilling across the darkness from down the road in the direction of a neighboring camp.

For Amy and Kirsty, this was straightforwardly annoying. They had come here for the sounds of the desert night — and there are sounds, if you're still enough to hear them. For me, I'll admit I was annoyed in one part of my brain and intrigued in another. The noise was inconsiderate, yes. But it was also, if I'm honest, an invitation. Not a formal one. But an invitation, nonetheless.

And I have never been good at ignoring those. I have a particular philosophy that has got me into both trouble and unexpected joy over the years: I will never see these people again, and so I have nothing to lose.

When Amy and Kirsty settled into their swags, I carefully assembled a cooler, grabbed my torch, and announced I was going to go and politely ask our neighbors to turn the music down so we could enjoy the night properly. This was not entirely untrue. I was planning to ask them to quiet the music.

Eventually.

After I'd had a look at the party.

Kirsty and Amy thought I was mad. I told them it was an important mission, and I would not let them down.

I set off into the dark with my cooler and my torch and what I can only describe as adventurous boldness, picking my way through the bush toward the music. I should note, with the benefit of hindsight, wandering alone through the Australian desert at night isn't the most sensible decision a person can make. The dark between campsites is a different dark than what you're used to. But not all good decisions are going to happen out here, and I made my peace with that.

When I arrived, the music did in fact turn down. Amy told me the next morning she'd laughed herself half to sleep, assuming my appearance had caused the volume reduction. The truth was somewhat more deflating: The music had dropped not because I'd asked anyone to turn it down, but because the assembled group was trying to work out who this strange person was, emerging from the dark desert in her pajama pants, carrying a cooler.

I introduced myself. I said I was there to wish someone either a happy birthday or congratulations, because this was clearly a kick-ass party. They had a DJ booth set up in the dry riverbed.

People had been dancing in the desert sand. It turned out to be someone's thirtieth birthday. I found this delightful.

I made my rounds, moved from one conversation to the next, tried my best to be a charming and unexpected addition to the evening. The welcome wasn't exactly overwhelming. There was a certain quality to the looks I received —a cross between intrigue and mild bewilderment —suggested I was perhaps not quite the party crasher who would blend seamlessly into the group. I read the room, or rather the riverbed, and made a hushed exit back into the dark.

Kirsty and Amy were still awake when I got back. They had a good laugh. I deserved it. Before I left the party, I did my civic duty and asked them to keep it a little quieter. They obliged. I counted that a partial success.

MORNING IN THE DESERT

The morning came the way desert mornings do — with birds first. Before the light fully arrives, the sound does. The desert waking up isn't hushed; it's layered and urgent and entirely its own kind of music, the kind no DJ booth in a dry riverbed could ever replicate or improve upon.

We made coffee in the cool air, sat with it for a while, and let the landscape do what it does — remind you the world is enormous and ancient. We packed up our swags from the red earth, loaded the ute, and made the beautiful drive back toward Alice Springs. The ranges watched us go.

I survived another night of swag camping in the desert. More than survived — I climbed a ridge that nearly stopped my heart, sat at the top of the world, breathed beauty into my bones, crashed a thirtieth birthday party in the dark, and woken to birdsong on red earth.

CHAPTER 14

THE CALL FROM THE SANCTUARY

This is where it all began.

At five a.m. on September 25, 2023, when the desert was still dark and restful — and I should have been asleep — I sent a message that would quietly change my time in Australia.

I told the sanctuary I moved to Alice Springs from the States. A month earlier, I toured the Kangaroo Sanctuary, paying attention as they described rescuing orphaned joeys and caring for them until they were strong enough to return to the wild. They spoke about training, commitment, responsibility.

A weight in me leaned forward.

So, before sunrise, I typed a careful, hopeful note. I introduced myself as a teacher. I explained I was new to town, admitted how completely interested I was and asked about training, and thanked them for any information they could share.

I had no idea this small, early-morning message — sent with sleepy eyes and a full heart — was the first step into a world of red dirt and a love for kangaroos I didn't yet understand.

THE AUTOMATED RESPONSE

I received an automated message in return:

> *"Thank you for your message.*
> *We receive a high volume of messages and try to reply to all, but sometimes we are unable to.*
>
> *Visiting our kangaroos: you can visit by pre-booking a guided tour at www.kangaroosanctuary.com*
>
> *Volunteering: Thank you for asking, but we don't have any vacant roles at the moment. If we do in the future, we will advertise on our website, Facebook, and Instagram pages.*
>
> *Take care,*
> *Tahnee & Brolga"*

It was polite. Efficient. Final.

ON OCTOBER 3, I TRIED AGAIN.

I sent the same message; hopeful it might land differently this time. Instead, I received the same automated response — polite, distant, impersonal.

It felt like shouting into the desert and hearing only my own echo return.

(Side note: Tahnee and Brolga, who run the Kangaroo Sanctuary, are among the busiest, most devoted people I can imagine. Their lives revolve around caring for dozens of rescued kangaroos — many requiring round-the-clock attention. They receive countless messages

daily. There's no judgment here. If anything, knowing that made me admire them more. It also made me more determined.)

Later that day, I sent another message — shorter this time, more direct. I tried not to sound impatient, but I couldn't hide my eagerness. I asked again about training.

This time, a real response arrived.

They thanked me for reaching out and confirmed they had received my message.

My heart leapt.

Without overthinking it, I replied immediately.

I told them I would love the opportunity to become a kangaroo mother. I promised — half joking, half completely serious —I would provide whatever care was needed. I would cuddle baby roos, give endless love and attention, and when the time came, do the hardest part: Let them go back to the wild where they belonged.

I explained how fully the mission mattered to me.

OCTOBER 4 MESSAGE

On October 4, I sent:

> *"My contact information is…*
> *I moved to Alice Springs from Iowa in June. It's been a dream of mine to teach in Australia. After twenty-four years of teaching in the States, I left everything behind to follow that dream. I'm currently teaching science at Larapinta Primary School. I'm happy to provide references. Please let me know how I can help support your mission."*

And then… nothing.

Days passed.

Excitement slowly transitioned into doubt.
Maybe they were overwhelmed.
Maybe my messages were disappearing.
Maybe this simply wasn't meant to be.

The silence felt heavier each day.

OCTOBER 10 — PERSISTENCE

On October 10, I tried again.

I asked if there were updates about training. The automated reply came instantly —known and disappointing.

Later that same day, I sent another message.

At this point, I figured I had nothing to lose. I would either convince them I was serious or get myself blocked on Facebook.

At least I would know.

11:11 P.M.

And then — on October 11, at exactly 11:11 p.m. — it happened.

A real message.
A real person.
A real answer.

I remember the moment vividly. My heart pounded as I read the words I had been waiting for.

They called me by name.

They explained the commitment — two days a week, minimum six months. They asked about my availability. They offered another pathway through Wildcare for in-home care.

I stared at the screen, smiling like a child who had been handed exactly what she'd wished for.

They wrote:

"Hi Becky. That's great you want to raise orphaned kangaroos... We require at least 2 days per week on a roster system and a minimum of 6 months..."

They explained the importance of raising at least two joeys together — so they could feel companionship, a heartbeat beside them, like they would in their mother's pouch.

That detail undid me.

A heartbeat they can feel.

After weeks of waiting, wondering, and sending messages into the unknown, the door had cracked open.

And I knew my time here was about to change.

I responded immediately.
No hesitation.
No checking my calendar.

Weekend shifts. I could start right away.

Their reply came quickly: Could I come Saturday for thirty minutes to meet them and see the sanctuary?

Later, Brolga would tell me the truth. With the number of messages I sent, he wanted to meet me first —to be sure I wasn't completely crazy.

Fair enough.

Apparently, I passed.

Because after that short visit — after they decided my enthusiasm was the manageable kind — I was given the green light.

I think I needed them to say yes—not solely for the kangaroos, but because I needed affirmation. I needed the confidence it would give me to keep going through a time that felt uncertain, to trust I was on the right path.

What began as early-morning hope and stubborn persistence had become real.

I hadn't been blocked.
I hadn't been ignored.
I had been welcomed.

The page had turned, and the dream that started at five a.m. in the dark was no longer a dream.

It was an invitation.

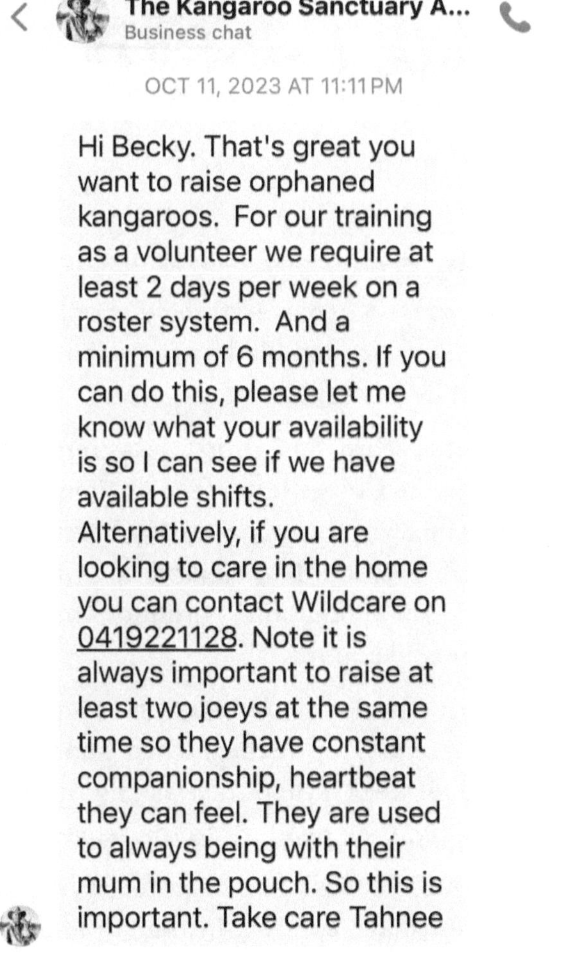

The Kangaroo Sanctuary A...
Business chat

OCT 11, 2023 AT 11:11 PM

Hi Becky. That's great you want to raise orphaned kangaroos. For our training as a volunteer we require at least 2 days per week on a roster system. And a minimum of 6 months. If you can do this, please let me know what your availability is so I can see if we have available shifts. Alternatively, if you are looking to care in the home you can contact Wildcare on 0419221128. Note it is always important to raise at least two joeys at the same time so they have constant companionship, heartbeat they can feel. They are used to always being with their mum in the pouch. So this is important. Take care Tahnee

CHAPTER 15

POUCHES, PEACE, AND PURPOSE

Volunteering at the sanctuary became my lifeline.

It gave me purpose when everything else still felt unsettled. It made me feel useful. Needed. And it offered an experience that could only happen in Australia.

There was a lot to learn, and at first, I was terrified of making mistakes— missing a step, forgetting a feeding time, not remembering the exact milk mixture for each joey. My shifts were Saturday and Sunday afternoons, and before long, my weekends settled into a steady flow. That predictability grounded me. It made Alice Springs begin to feel like home.

Saturday mornings always unfolded the same way. I'd wake up, start a load of laundry, tackle the kitchen, and finally wash the dishes I'd ignored all week. When the washing finished, I'd hang my clothes out to dry, then head off to the sanctuary.

Leah trained me. She was American too, living in Australia, and there was immediate comfort in that. We spoke the same language — not merely English, but the same sarcasm. It felt good to be understood without explanation.

I usually arrived around 12:30, as Leah was finishing feedings and bathroom breaks with the joeys. I jumped straight into the laundry, which was never small. Every joey snuggled inside a pillowcase nestled into a pouch — their version of their mother's warmth and safety. My first job was to shake out each pouch, making sure every last bit of poo was gone before throwing them into the wash. There were endless towels too, because helping kangaroos go to the bathroom is messy work.

When the washing finished, everything went straight onto the clothesline. That short walk outside always made me slightly uneasy. Opening the door felt like stepping into the unknown, aware that in this remote part of Australia, plenty of elements could kill you if you weren't paying attention. I stayed alert — hanging laundry, spending time with the roos in the yard, as well as when I crossed paths with Beatrice the camel. Snakes were always in the back of my mind.

After the laundry came the dishes — an endless number of bottles needed to be scrubbed and ready for the next feed. All of it happened while the roos slept, bellies full of milk, tucked away and peaceful.

And in those gentle pauses— folding, washing, hanging, cleaning — a feeling evolved.

For the first time in a long time, I felt at peace.

There were no worries about what everyone else was doing or what I might be missing on Facebook. No anxiety about reality TV, my clothes, or how I looked. I wasn't thinking about nail appointments or sales at Von Maur. There was no pressure to keep up with TikTok trends, Amazon lightning deals, or the constant pull to buy, want, and accumulate more.

The endless chatter in my head softened. The comparisons. The measuring myself against others. The silent fear I was never quite enough.

In the stillness, the noise faded.

I was simply present.

And the more I sat in that feeling, the more I started to understand where it was coming from.

This wasn't the type of "busy" I was used to. There was no recognition, no outcome to showcase, no visible reward waiting at the end. The work was repetitive, gentle, and often unseen. And yet, it felt more meaningful than so many of the tasks that used to fill my time.

It wasn't about me.

Caring for the kangaroos provided a strange sort of freedom. It was about showing up for a task that required consistency rather than perfection. They didn't need me to be impressive. They didn't need me to be anything other than present and reliable. And in that, all the pressure I had been carrying without realizing it started to fall away.

So much of my life had been shaped by keeping up—keeping up with expectations, with appearances, with what everyone else seemed to be doing. Still when I tried to slow down, my mind didn't. It was always scanning, comparing, evaluating.

But here, that pattern didn't follow me in the same way.

There was no space for comparison when your hands were full and your attention was needed right in front of you. No reason to think about what you lacked when what you were doing felt enough.

And maybe, that's what changed.

I wasn't chasing anything.
I wasn't trying to prove anything.
I was just… contributing.

In a way that felt quiet, steady, and real.

And now I find myself wondering what happens when this ends.

Because this version of life—this version of me—feels different. Lighter. Less tangled in worries that used to feel important.

I know I'll return to a world that moves faster, pulls for attention in a hundred different directions. But maybe I don't have to meet it the same way I did before.

Maybe I can be more intentional about what I give my energy to.
Maybe I can choose moments of presence over distraction.
Maybe I can see things differently now—and not lose that perspective.

I don't know exactly how that will look yet.

But I do know this feeling is a feeling I don't want to lose.

SUNSHINE AND HOPS

Eventually, it was time to let the kangaroos go outside for a hop.

I began to understand the sanctuary was carefully organized in stages — each yard representing a different chapter in a kangaroo's journey.

Some kangaroos lived there full-time, unable to be released back into the bush at around a year old. Sometimes they'd been injured when their mother was killed. Other times, they'd bonded so closely with a buddy who couldn't be released that separating them would have been too traumatic. These were the kangaroos visitors met on tours — safe, cared for, permanent residents.

Another section held kangaroos almost ready for freedom. Volunteers didn't interact with them at all. The goal was for them to relearn fear of humans, so they'd have the best chance of surviving in the wild.

Nearby were slightly smaller roos who lived outside full-time but weren't quite independent yet. Then there was the yard closest to the sanctuary — a mob spent their days outside, coming in at night or slipping inside for an afternoon nap. Some still drank bottles; others had transitioned to greens and grains.

And finally, there were the smallest — the newest rescues. On average, about a dozen. Some were under six months old and lived entirely in their pouches, not yet strong enough to hop. Others could manage a few shaky jumps before scrambling back inside. The older joeys, around six months, hopped confidently around the yard after feeding but always returned to the pouch for comfort and sleep.

For the tiniest roos who couldn't go outside yet, there was another essential task: helping them go to the bathroom. This meant gently placing them on a towel and rubbing their bottom until they peed — and ultimately pooped. In the wild, their mother would lick them to stimulate the process. At the sanctuary, we used our hands instead.

I imagine this is where some people would politely excuse themselves and decide volunteering wasn't for them.

It certainly wasn't my favorite task.

But it was necessary.

My favorite moments were taking the smaller joeys outside for sunshine during the cooler months. I'd load them into a laundry basket, each tucked snugly into their pouch, and carry them to a sunny patch of yard. They'd sleep in the basket while I held them one by one.

It's hard to explain what that felt like — sitting in the desert sun with a kangaroo in my arms, taking in the sound of galahs calling overhead.

It was a peace I had never known.

Completely relaxed. Genuinely happy. Free from stress, worry, guilt, and shame.

At that moment, the only thing that mattered was the joey in my arms — the one who now saw me as their mum. And caring for them stirred feeling layered somewhere within me. A reminder of who I am at my core: steady, nurturing, capable of giving love without needing anything in return.

After sunshine and hops came bottle time. Sometimes twenty or more at once, each mixed to a different strength. The milk had to be warmed — and, unfortunately, tasted to make sure it was right. My least favorite part.

The smallest joeys were fed individually. Some drank quickly; others took their sweet time. The bigger ones could be fed two at once from their pouches inside the laundry basket. The outside mob was fed together, and over time I mastered feeding about eight joeys at once.

When the feedings ended, my afternoon continued with more laundry, more bottles, and more cuddles until Brolga arrived to take over for the night.

Then there was Beatrice, a camel rescued when she was still very young, not yet able to survive on her own without her mother.

Feeding her meant mixing camel formula in a large bowl, pouring it into a two-liter bottle fitted with a nipple, and driving down a bumpy, twisting path to her paddock. As soon as I pulled up, she knew. She'd pace the fence, making impatient, insistent noises, demanding her bottle.

Once she latched on, you had to be ready. Her suction was so strong the nipple would pop right off.

I grew to love her — the slobber, the sounds, the sheer presence she brought to every interaction.

And then there was Tahnee, Brolga's wife—the camel whisperer, able to tell exactly what they needed and caring for them with the kind of love a mother gives her only child.

Watching her changed me.

I've never met anyone with such profound love for animals, nature, and the serene beauty of life. She notices everything. She absorbs it. She invites others to slow down and do the same. Calm. Grounded. Giving.

Being around her encouraged me to move through the world differently — slower, more attentive, more aware of the small sacred details most of us rush past.

Journal Entry — 10/21/23

It's Saturday morning, and my heart is happy. I love my new home and having the kangaroos visit every day. I love the peaceful sounds of nature. I miss my family and friends, but my heart is happy here too.

I wake up, water the roos that visit my veranda, wash the laundry, and hang it out to dry. It's a simple, peaceful way of life, and I love it. It reminds me of Little House on the Prairie, one of my all-time favorite shows.

At five today, I'm heading to the Kangaroo Sanctuary to meet Chris and Tahnee. I'm so excited. Australia brings me such an immense sense of peace. I wonder why that is — and how I can carry this feeling home with me.

I love having a small space and how easy it is to keep clean. What I need is to simplify my life when I return. Less clutter. More intention. More time to journal. More stillness and meditation.

Why do I feel so happy today?

My emotions feel relaxed, grounded, at peace — and I want to remember this forever.

Please never forget this truth: The best feelings in life don't come from eating, drinking, or shopping—they come from something deeper.

Right now, happiness looks like country music playing softly, eating an apple, and watching nature outside my window.

Anything is possible.

I need to slow down and truly enjoy my life.

Brad may get his dream of us living in a camper and spending our summer in Parkersburg at Beaver Meadows Golf Course. Be ready, P-Burg peeps!

Reflecting on it now, volunteering at the sanctuary was about so much more than feeding joeys and washing endless piles of laundry.

It was therapy.
It was harmony.
It slowed my racing thoughts and reminded me what truly matters.

Each task — folding towels, hanging pouches, scrubbing bottles — showed me joy isn't found in noise or busyness, but in meaningful work and real connection. Surrounded by animals who depended on us, I learned how to simply be.

For the first time in a long time, I wasn't chasing happiness through material comforts or distractions.

I found it — under the desert sun, in the stillness between kangaroo heartbeats, in the silent knowing I was exactly where I was meant to be.

And in that space, I came to understand a lesson simple and profound: Happiness isn't what you chase.

It's how you feel when you choose what brings you joy.

Getting ready to feed the kangaroos, wearing my fly net.

Beatrice and I.

CHAPTER 16:
MY NEW BEGINNING

KANGAROO RELEASE — 11/6/23

A feeling awakened this weekend.

The kangaroo release alone would have made it unforgettable. My heart pounded the entire drive out, determined not to make a mistake. I sat between James and Brolga as he narrated the red desert like a storyteller, pointing out landmarks and memories stitched into the land. When bikers appeared ahead of us, he leaned on the horn and joked if he hit one, "we saw nothing."

Dark Aussie humor — oddly comforting in the tension.

But the moment the kangaroos bounded into open country silenced everything. Watching them disappear into freedom was breathtaking. They moved with strength and certainty, vanishing into land that had always been theirs. There was a holiness about it—a conclusion final and right.

As they grew smaller against the horizon, a heavy, bittersweet ache settled in my chest. I felt a surge of pure, radiant happiness that they were finally home—that they were free to be exactly what they were meant to be. But right on its heels came the sharp sting of reality: I would never see them again. The hands that had bottled-fed them and the heart that had sheltered them were no longer needed.

And as I stood there, I slowly began to see, I wasn't purely watching the kangaroos.

I was noticing how tightly I'd been holding myself, carrying expectations and pressures that weren't truly mine. So much of my life had been spent performing, trying to meet imagined standards and obligations. Seeing the kangaroos bound across the red earth, I felt a gentle urge to let some of that go — to relax, to breathe, to simply be present without rushing or worrying.

I couldn't stop watching. The way they leapt and disappeared into the open desert stirred a part in me. Not a realization or a plan, a feeling: the simple, unspoken desire to let myself move through life a little more lightly, to notice what's around me instead of filling the stillness with constant motion.

I didn't need to perform, to impress, or to prove anything. I wanted to exist in the space I was in, fully aware, fully present, like they were. That image stayed with me, lingering softly long after the kangaroos had gone.

Journal Entry — 11/7/23

Derby Day in Alice Springs is nothing like the Kentucky Derby.

It's relaxed, slightly chaotic, and gloriously unpolished. No one tries too hard. People dress up for the fun of it, laugh easily, and let the day unfold as it will.

Between the races and the afterparty, I acquired the nickname "USA." It stuck instantly.

Alice Springs feels like a hippy town suspended in the '80s — loose, imperfect, unconcerned with appearances. I love that about it. There is no pressure to fit in, no unspoken rules about how you should look or present yourself. Some people dress up; others don't—but no one seems to notice or care. Everyone is ... themselves—and this is the expectation.

This area makes me feel alive.

And that's what complicates everything.

The more at home I feel under this endless desert sky, the more I miss the people who are my heart back in Iowa. How do you choose between a place that awakens you and the people who raised you? Half of me feels rooted in this red dirt. The other half is still at home — with my family, my friends, my pets, even my plants.

Growth, I'm learning, can feel exhilarating and painful at the same time.

Journal Entry — 11/9/23

Tonight, the pieces of the journey finally seemed to click together on their own. Since arriving here, I've learned how to love myself. Writing that feels strange—almost uncomfortable—but it's true.

Sitting alone, listening to the music drift through the donga, I caught myself thinking that maybe coming all this way had been reckless. But then, a stronger thought followed: No. It was brave. It took courage to leave comfort behind. Courage to risk looking foolish. Courage to stretch far beyond the life I once knew. Instead of falling back into my usual habit of self-criticism, I felt a wave of genuine pride.

There's something incredibly freeing about recognizing your own growth. Maybe this is how love is supposed to work— starting from the inside. Earlier, I caught myself thinking, "She's someone I actually like." And I stopped. I had never thought that about myself. Not once.

For most of my life, I focused on everything I wasn't— prettier, thinner, smarter, better. I was constantly chasing the ghost of a "better" version of myself: a better mom, a better daughter, a better sister, a better wife. The list was endless, and so was the quiet disappointment that followed it. But at some point in this red dust, that transformed. I looked at the woman in the mirror and realized I finally respected her. I liked the way she handled the heat, the way she cared for the animals, and the way she stood her ground.

I see how far I've come now—not in a loud or bragging way, but in a quiet, steady knowing. Loving yourself doesn't mean announcing it to the world; it means no longer carrying a constant sense of failure. A few nights ago, I told my parents I missed them. Then, through tears, I told them I was proud of myself—that I loved myself. They didn't quite know what to say. But I think they understood.

Being here has stripped life back to the essentials. Without the usual noise and roles to hide behind, I've had to meet myself honestly. Each challenge has taught me about the world, about life, and about who I am when everything else is taken away. I've learned I don't need all the "extras" to feel happy or loved. What I needed was simplicity. Vulnerability. Space to rediscover myself without distraction.

November 9, 2023.

A turning point.

My new beginning.

CHAPTER 17:
RESILIENT THINGS

Journal Entry — 11/19/23

It's Sunday morning, and I'm getting ready to head to the Kangaroo Sanctuary.

Volunteering there has become the anchor of my weekends. It gives my days shape — moments steady and purposeful. It lets me care for animals, do good work, and help in ways that feel meaningful and real. The sanctuary has quietly become part of me. I am incredibly grateful for the opportunity to be there.

This week, though, carries a heaviness.

Thanksgiving is coming, and being away from my family presses harder against my heart than usual. I keep reminding myself why I'm here — the promise I made to myself, the strength it took to come. Christmas is only a few weeks away. I can hold on until then.

Still, this Thanksgiving feels different. Slower. More reflective. For the first time, gratitude isn't rushed between dishes and conversations. I've always had these blessings, but here I've been given space to truly notice them.

The gift of slowing down. Of stepping back. Of really seeing my life.

My heart feels full, and I hope I carry this gratitude long after this journey ends.

Now it's time for the sanctuary — and my little roos.

Journal Entry — 11/27/23

Another weekend gone — and two new arrivals at the Kangaroo Sanctuary: Wobble and Rodney.

Wobble is gentle and curious, surprisingly calm for a newcomer. Rodney is still settling in. There are hopeful wishes about new rescues. Each one carries a story we may never fully know, but here they are given a second chance.

On Sunday evening, I brought chips and beer (for me) to Jackie's house. We spent the evening talking, the conversations that feel unfiltered and honest. That seems to happen often here. Maybe it's the desert. Maybe it's how life is stripped back. There is less performance. More truth.

Lately, I've been thinking about how to explain Alice Springs to people.

Some describe it as rough. Broken. Dangerous.

And yes — Alice carries heavy realities. Racism. Generational trauma. Alcohol and drug abuse. Youth crime. The kinds of systemic wounds that do not heal quickly.

So, it's fair to ask: Why here?

But that is only one side of the story.

Alice is also filled with people whose hearts are impossibly big. People who show up every day to serve others. Who fight for this town. Who believe in it, when it would be easier not to.

I have met people who would give their last dollar to someone in need without hesitation.

Alice is raw and imperfect — but fiercely loved by those who call it home.

And then there is the beauty.

The red dirt. The mountain ranges. The dry riverbeds and gum trees. Wildlife everywhere you look — the calls of galahs and red-winged black cockatoos, the low rhythmic drumbeat of emus moving through the evening air.

There truly is no other place like Alice.

To never experience it — to never feel its complexity, its magic, its contradictions — would be a loss.

11/29/23 — WHAT NOT TO DO WHEN YOU SEE A SNAKE

I encountered an extremely venomous snake while walking students to class.

Instead of staying calm and guiding the students inside, my reaction was straight out of an action movie. My heart raced, adrenaline surged, and I screamed "Snake!" at the top of my lungs, telling the students to run for their lives.

Thankfully, everything turned out fine. The snake catcher was called and safely relocated the snake. Once we got back to my classroom, the principal came in to speak to the students, reminding them when they see a snake, they should remain calm and not run. One student politely raised his hand and said, "Mrs. K told us to run."

He was right. I had been called out by an eight-year-old, and the only thing I could do was admit my mistake, blame it on being American, and promise next time I would hopefully remain calm myself. My reaction got a good laugh from the staff, and once again, I owned another experience where I could laugh at myself. I am fairly confident I will now be used as an example of what **not** to do when teachers see a snake.

At the same time, it was a sharp wake-up call. After the incident, talking with another teacher, I learned how serious a snake bite by an eastern brown could be —there are only about ten minutes to reach a hospital for antivenom before the consequences could be fatal. It was also hard to comprehend Australians don't kill venomous snakes when they see them. Instead, they call the snake catcher, who shows up in flip-flops, carefully takes the snake, and releases it back into the bush.

I was shocked. Any American I know would have killed that snake without a second thought. And yet, knowing how deadly it could be, there's an intense respect for nature — a recognition the snake has as much right to be on the land as we humans do. It was a moment unexpectedly beautiful.

I do have to admit, though, after the encounter, I called my husband. An enormous wave of emotion hit me as the truth settled into me how dangerous this place can be. Australia is a country where sometimes it feels like everything is actively trying to kill you.

It's home to twenty-one of the twenty-five most venomous snakes in the world. The Sydney funnel-web—the deadliest spider. Sharks. Crocodiles the size of a car. The blue-ringed octopus—tiny and beautiful—but able to kill you in minutes. A cone snail that looks harmless but is highly venomous. Bull ants whose aggressive sting can trigger severe reactions. Including caterpillars you have to watch out for because they can cause the same type of reaction.

There's a plant that, if you brush against it, can cause so much pain it makes you want to throw yourself off a cliff—and that pain can last for weeks, even months. A dinosaur-like bird that can rip you apart with its feet.

And there's the sun—some of the highest UV levels in the world—like it's trying to kill you too.

I couldn't think of anything in Iowa that could kill you with one small bite, and that realization was overwhelming.

Journal Entry — 12/3/23

I experienced a fantastic weekend at the Kangaroo Sanctuary.

Brolga shared a touching story about a kangaroo named Timmy.

Brolga raised Timmy from the time he was a tiny pinkie. One day, Brolga came home and found Timmy lying lifeless on the ground. Though Timmy still had air in his lungs, he was in a coma.

Timmy spent four days at the vet on life support, costing nearly $1,000 per day.

One the fourth day, an incredible change happened.

Timmy woke up.

The vet feared brain damage, but to everyone's surprise, he began hopping again that same day.

Because of his medical history and miraculous recovery, Brolga decided Timmy would stay at the sanctuary and when the moment came, take on a special role — becoming the next king, succeeding Roger.

Roger had been the sanctuary's famous alpha male, appearing in several television productions. Brolga often joked about having to run from Roger's powerful presence.

Recently, Timmy — who has not yet been neutered — challenged Brolga for the first time. Brolga wasn't sure this moment would come so soon, but he believes Timmy is ready to step into Roger's role.

This all happened before the film 'Kangaroo' was announced. The filmmakers were looking for a strong, dominant male kangaroo like Roger — and Timmy is growing into that role perfectly.

I admire Brolga's devotion — not just to the animals, but to helping people understand them.

Kangaroos are resilient. Adaptable. Built for this landscape. They adjust. They survive. They keep moving forward.

In many ways, so do the people who choose to stay here and care for them.

Maybe that is what keeps drawing me back every weekend.

It's not only the animals.

It's the reminder strength does not have to be loud.

Sometimes strength looks like showing up — again and again.

CHAPTER 18:
BETWEEN TWO HOMES

Journal Entry — 12/14/23

Today is my last day of school before I head home to Iowa for Christmas.

I've started to pack. My laundry is done — or at least started. In three days, I'll be on a plane.

I worry about flying. I worry about missing Alice — my friends, my routines, the kangaroos who have tenderly claimed my heart.

And I worry when I'm home in Iowa, surrounded by family and routines, I won't be fully present. Part of me will already be bracing for the return trip, anticipating the loneliness of readjusting to life so far away from them.

When the worry gets loud, I try to remember why I came here.

One of the clearest reasons was to find my sense of adventure again. I used to be brave without trying. Curious without overthinking. Over time, that version of me became quieter.

This trip isn't about running away.
It's about calling myself back home — wherever home turns out to be.

Journal Entry — 12/16/23

Tomorrow, I leave for Sydney.

Today is my last day at the Kangaroo Sanctuary for six weeks, and the weight of that feels heavier than I expected.

I keep asking myself the same question: Is it possible for two places to feel like home?

And if it is, does that mean I will always feel homesick? That no matter where I stand, part of me will always be longing for the place I am not?

Journal Entry — 1/6/24

I have been back at home in Iowa for three weeks, and reverse culture shock is dreadfully real.

I notice it everywhere.

Life in America feels louder, faster, fuller. People are consumed by choices, by possessions, by their phones. My anxiety has increased since arriving home, and I think I know why.

My house feels too full. Too many objects. Too many decisions. My nervous system doesn't know where to rest.

At the same time, I carry fear about returning to Alice — about how hard it will be to leave Iowa again. Being home is wonderful. Seeing everyone has filled my heart. And oh, how I have missed my dog, Ozzie.

I came across a quote that resonated fully with me:

> *"Start paying attention to your glimmers, because they are the opposite of your triggers. They are the small moments of peace or joy that help our nervous system feel safe and connected."*
>
> *(author unknown)*

I hold onto that idea as I navigate this strange in-between space.

Being home after seven months away has highlighted how much my lifestyle has changed. I love laughing with old friends and hugging my family in person. But I feel overwhelmed by stores, endless aisles, and too many choices.

I have realized I prefer a simpler life with fewer decisions.

And I do appreciate being able to use the toilet without first checking for snakes.

There's also a quieter grief I didn't expect.

I've realized people aren't always as eager to hear my stories as I am to share them. Maybe it's because some experiences are difficult to relate to unless you've lived them, or maybe they simply don't hold the same meaning for others.

Some experiences change you in ways that cannot always be translated.

The busyness here feels different — almost frantic. People seem constantly rushed, driven by schedules, spending, and doing.

And almost immediately, I felt old habits pulling at me. The urge to buy. The excitement of a good deal. That known, uneasy pull toward wanting objects simply because they exist.

It is frightening how quickly old patterns can return.

But awareness gives me choice.

I know what I need.
I need to write more.
To process.

To document the gentle changes happening within me.

I need meditation. Stillness. Practices that help me stay grounded when my heart is stretched across continents.

Maybe this is what adventure looks like now.

Not constant movement.
But learning to live between places.
Between versions of myself.

Maybe having two homes doesn't mean I will always feel lost.

Maybe it means my heart is wide enough to hold both.

Journal Entry — 1/23/24

Tomorrow morning, I leave for Australia again.

My bags are ready, but my heart feels split open.

I am carrying guilt, worry, and excitement all at once.

Leaving will be hard. Saying goodbye to Brad weighs heavily on me, especially if he cries. That image alone makes me emotional.

Saying goodbye to my friends and family will be a little easier than the first time — but "easier" doesn't mean easy.

It will still hurt.

What I do know is this: This is a once-in-a-lifetime experience. I don't want to look back and feel like I merely survived it instead of truly living it.

I want to experience everything — not in a perfect, picture-perfect way, but in a real way. The kind that includes fear, growth, and stretching beyond comfort.

I have asked myself a difficult but necessary question: Would I rather stay here in the dead of winter, working in a safe but anxiety-driven world? Or return to adventure — gather memories that change me, and return with stories that matter?

The answer is clear.

Going back to Australia gives me perspective. It helps me discover my next steps — my next job, my next version of myself. It helps me learn how to manage anxiety instead of letting it control me.

> *If I stay, I know what would happen. I would feel stuck. Disappointed in myself. Not because I'm weak, but because comfort can become dangerous when it keeps us from growing.*
>
> *I don't want to chase happiness through possessions anymore.*
>
> *I want presence. Boldness. Connection. Self-respect.*
>
> *I need to learn how to focus on what truly matters.*
>
> *Tomorrow, I choose the unknown.*
>
> *Not because I am fearless.*
>
> *But because I am willing to live with fear without letting it control my life.*

WHEN FEAR ISN'T IN CHARGE

There's a difference between feeling fear and living in it.

For a long time, I didn't realize how much of my life was shaped by it. Not the loud, obvious kind—but the muted kind that keeps you comfortable, predictable, safe. The kind that sounds like being practical. Responsible. Logical.

I chose what felt safe. I stayed where life made sense. And over time, I built a life that worked—but didn't fully feel like mine.

Coming to Australia was the first time I made a decision that didn't revolve around avoiding fear. There were no guarantees, no clear outcome, no reassurance I was doing the "right" thing.

And that was the point.

For the first time, I chose this because it challenged me. It forced me out of my carefully constructed life and into uncharted territory

Fear didn't disappear. It's still there.

But it's no longer in charge.

And it's possible, that's the shift—not becoming fearless, but choosing to live anyway.

Journal Entry — 1/28/24

I have been back in Australia for three days, and the transition has been harder than I expected.

I cannot seem to find my groove again. I didn't feel entirely happy at home, and I don't feel entirely happy here either. That realization scares me more than I want to admit.

Will I ever truly be happy?

And what is wrong with me for asking that question?

Why can't I settle? Why does my heart always feel divided between places, people, and versions of myself?

The thought of going months without seeing Brad breaks my heart — for me and for him. I want both of us to be happy, and sometimes I don't know how to make that happen.

There are moments when I wish I had never come here. I wish I hadn't chosen this discomfort, this loneliness, this constant emotional stretching.

I miss home. I miss my girls. I miss my dogs. I miss sleeping next to Brad.

And yet, another truth exists alongside that pain.

There are parts of this life here I genuinely love.

I love the simplicity.

I love taking care of responsibilities myself.

I don't miss the pressure of maintaining a large house or carrying responsibilities that once felt overwhelming.

I've found a home in this stillness.

I love that decisions are mine alone. I can watch TV or not. Journal or meditate without explanation. Sit in stillness without needing permission.

That freedom is grounding.

Both truths exist at the same time — and that is what makes this so complicated.

I live with uncertainty now. Some days it feels unbearable.

But I also know this is a once-in-a-lifetime journey. I don't want to spend it wishing it away.

This is my time to learn who I am when I cannot escape my emotions.

To grow.

To reflect.

To sit with discomfort instead of running from it.

I may not have everything figured out.

I may not feel happiness the way I once thought I would.

But I believe in myself.

I believe I can do what seems impossible.

This journey is shaping me —including when it hurts.

Or perhaps the question isn't whether I will ever feel truly happy in a constant, unchanging way. Maybe that was never the point.

I think I've been looking at happiness as a destination, I'm supposed to arrive at—a sense of stillness I can reach once everything feels settled.

But I'm not settled. I'm growing.

I'm changing in ways I don't fully understand yet, and it could be that's why my path feels uncertain. I'm not the same person I was before I left, and I'm not fully who I'm becoming yet either. I'm at a stage in the process.

Perhaps happiness doesn't live in a final version of me—it exists in this process of becoming.

Maybe happiness comes in waves—sometimes strong, sometimes quiet, sometimes hidden beneath discomfort. We expect it to be constant, or to arrive quickly, but it doesn't work that way.

What I do know is I don't want to stay stagnant—held back by fear, choosing comfort over growth. Because it's in the growth, in the change, in facing fear and doing the challenges that stretch me, that's when I truly feel alive.

Happiness isn't instant. It's a process.

And it could be, that's the lesson I'm starting to understand— the same process that brought me here—the uncertainty, the pull, the willingness to step into the unknown—is the very process I need to trust to find happiness and peace.

I've got this.

CHAPTER 19

SHOULD I STAY, OR SHOULD I GO?

February was when the question stopped being hushed.

It no longer sat politely in the background, waiting for the right moment. It followed me—through the classroom, across the red dirt, into my evenings, and into the stillness of night.

Should I stay, or should I go?

At first, it showed up in small ways.

At the kangaroo sanctuary, I found myself worrying about Bella, one of the joeys who didn't seem quite right. Brolga shared joeys are extremely vulnerable when they're young and prone to infections. She wasn't drinking her milk the way she should, and sometimes she would pull away from the others, isolating herself in a way that felt... off. Brolga wasn't sure what it meant—whether Bella was becoming independent, getting sick, or simply not thriving.

That uncertainty sat heavy with me.

We were doing everything we could for these animals, but there was a quiet truth we all understood: No matter how much care we gave, we could never fully replace what their mothers would have done naturally.

Sometimes care isn't enough to guarantee an outcome.

Sometimes you do your best and wait.

Now that time has passed, I think that's what unsettled me most—not Bella's fragility, but the reminder not everything can be controlled or fixed. Some things—health, growth, direction—unfold on their own timeline.

Much like my own life.

In the middle of the quiet reflections, there were also reminders of how unpredictable life in the Outback could be.

I learned a brown snake had gotten into the sanctuary through a small hole in the wall—a detail, in Australia, is explained almost casually. Snakes go into walls to catch mice. It's part of life here. Another volunteer had been sitting on the couch when he saw a snake poke its head out of the wall. The way the story was told, you'd think it was nothing out of the ordinary.

Another volunteer at the sanctuary had her own encounter, spotting a brown snake while hanging clothes on the line.

Moments like that made it impossible to forget where I was. Life here carried a different awareness—one where the ordinary could shift quickly into the unexpected.

And yet, right alongside the uncertainty and the edge of unpredictability, there was also excitement building.

Brolga shared April would be busy, with filming set to begin for a movie at the sanctuary. He talked about fifty to a hundred vehicles coming onto the paddock, full film crews, catering set up on-site. It felt surreal—this quiet space I had been spending time in suddenly becoming part of an event much bigger.

I found myself feeling a spark of excitement. I hoped I might get the chance to watch it all unfold—maybe be part of it in some small way.

That would be amazing.

2/4/24 — AUSSIE BLOKE PARTY

That same weekend, I went to Darrell's party.

Darrell was the custodian at school, the person every teacher knows is essential. He knew everything—how the building worked, what needed fixing, who needed help. Most afternoons, he would come into my classroom to collect the trash, but instead of rushing out, he'd pull up a chair and stay to talk.

Or, more accurately, he'd talk—and I'd do my best to follow along.

His Australian accent was one of the strongest I encountered, and I often found myself nodding, smiling, and piecing together whatever fragments I could understand. Occasionally, I would catch the gist of a story, but more often, I was along for the ride.

So, when he invited me to his party, insisting I come to see his band play, it felt easier to say yes than to explain why I might not.

The night of the party, I almost didn't go. But I reminded myself why I came to Australia. I hadn't come all this way to live the same life in a different location.

So I went. Alone.

Walking up his long driveway, hearing the music before I could see the people, I felt that obvious wave of uncertainty. The kind that makes you question your decisions halfway through carrying them out.

The crowd was a mix of personalities—some welcoming, some curious, some completely uninterested. At one point, someone told me they thought I had an Irish accent. I wasn't sure if it was my voice or my red hair that led them there.

I sat for a while, tried to make conversation, observed more than I spoke. At one table, people casually rolled joints, which prompted me to quietly relocate. I had seen enough episodes of *Locked Up Abroad* to know I didn't want to be sitting too close to anything questionable. I found my way to the food table instead, scanning for anything that looked recognizable, trying to avoid lamb, which seemed to be everywhere in Australia and nowhere near my list of favorites.

The music played on. Some songs I recognized, most I didn't. A few people sang along passionately, clearly having followed Darrell's band for years.

I didn't stay long.

I still felt like I didn't belong. That hadn't changed.

But something else had.

I went anyway.

Because the past version of me might have stayed on the couch talked herself out of it. But this version was learning to step into discomfort, even when it felt awkward, even when she didn't quite belong.

And I began to wonder if that same reserved strength would be required for the bigger decision waiting for me.

2/16/24 — THE WHIP SNAKE SHUFFLE

In Alice Springs, everyone seemed to have Rex's number saved in their phone. Rex was the local snake catcher — a man permanently on speed dial across this remote part of Australia. When someone spotted a snake Rex was the person they called.

His days were spent answering one call after another, driving across town and out into the surrounding desert to capture and relocate some of the most venomous snakes in the world. Some days, the calls were prioritized by the type of snake and where it had been spotted. A snake near a school or another highly populated area quickly moved to the top of the list.

One afternoon at school, we had another snake sighting — right at dismissal. It was a whip snake, not venomous enough to kill humans, but it would still hurt badly and require hospital treatment.

Instead of students pouring out the usual gates and pathways, teachers quickly redirected them along a different route while the area was cleared. In an area like Alice Springs, schools have a clear protocol when a snake is spotted: One person calls Rex, and another person keeps their eyes on the snake.

That day, I was brave enough to volunteer to be one of the "lucky ones."

We stood a cautious distance away, watching carefully as the snake slithered along the walkway between the classroom doors, clearly searching for an area to hide. Every so often, it would pause, lift its head slightly, and continue gliding forward.

Briefly, we tried to gently influence its direction by having someone stand a few feet ahead of it, hoping to block its path and keep it in a more open area until Rex arrived.

But the snake seemed to know the school grounds better than we did.

It slipped away from us and made its way toward the pumpkin patch near the edge of the school yard. The patch was thick with sprawling vines, broad leaves, and plenty of shaded places to disappear.

By the time Rex arrived — stepping out of his truck in flip-flops with his snake hook in hand — the snake had vanished into the tangled greenery.

He looked around the patch for a while, moving vines aside and scanning the ground, but there were simply too many places for it to hide. Finally, he shrugged slightly, explaining once a snake disappears into dense vegetation finding it can become nearly impossible.

The school day was already over, and Rex still had a long list of calls waiting for him.

So he climbed back into his truck, flip-flops and snake hook and all, and headed off to the next snake.

Living in the Outback has a way of teaching you realities you didn't ask to learn.

Like how easily a snake can find its way into a home.

Or how often they do.

I started hearing stories everywhere—snakes in garages, under couches, behind toilets, stretched across driveways, tucked beneath playground equipment. At first, they sounded like rare occurrences. But over time, it became clear to me, they weren't rare at all.

They were ... unseen.

Hidden.

Waiting.

Learning how deadly many Australian snakes are didn't exactly calm my nerves either. Some species can deliver venom that acts frighteningly fast, and once you know that, it's hard not to think about it.

The reassuring part is only a handful of people in Australia actually die from snake bites. Australians grow up learning to be "snake smart." You don't try to move the snake yourself. You don't approach it. You give it space and call someone like Rex.

Still, snakes slowly became a constant background thought that followed me through my days.

I thought about them when I lifted the lid of the toilet. When I stepped out of my car. When I unlocked the classroom in the morning. When I walked across the playground during duty. When I opened the door to my donga.

Sometimes I thought about them when I was trying to sleep.

Because another thing you learn living in the Outback is snakes occasionally make their way inside homes. And if a door is left open, briefly, a warm bed can look like an inviting place to settle in for the night.

Once that thought enters your mind, it's hard to shake.

Just like the question I can't seem to escape: *Should I stay or should I go?*

THE HEART OF HOME

Some days, the question felt exciting.

Other days, it felt heavy.

There were moments when I loved the simplicity of my life here—the independence, the quiet, the way my time belonged entirely to me. In the United States, my days had been filled with responsibilities—family schedules, constant decision-making, the invisible mental load of managing a household.

Here, everything was lighter.

But lightness came with absence.

I missed my family deeply. My husband. My girls. Including the dogs. The quiet that felt freeing during the day could feel painfully lonely at night.

My family is such a big part of my life, and each of them brings unique qualities that shapes the family dynamic.

Brooke, our firstborn, is the one who made me a mom. She carries a mix of Brad and me — a huge heart and intense compassion for others, a natural sense of what needs to happen. She loves being with family and staying busy, always making sure everyone around her has what they need. Sometimes she worries more about the happiness of others than her own. Brooke has a rare gift for connecting with people — she can talk honestly, relate deeply, and make others feel seen and understood.

Then there's Brinlee, one of the twins. She is much like her dad in her easygoing nature. Relaxed, go-with-the-flow, she has a calm presence that balances the chaos of life. She possesses unshakeable empathy, a gift for understanding, and often gives advice that considers the bigger picture. Brinlee naturally brings a sense of calmness and steadiness, making her the anchor in hectic moments.

Baylee, the other twin, is more like me — fiercely determined and motivated. She knows exactly what she wants and isn't afraid to speak up when she disagrees. Her confidence and clarity of purpose are inspiring; she faces challenges head-on and always advocates for herself and others.

Even though I love the freedom of being on my own, thinking about each of them — their strengths, their quirks, the ways they make life richer — makes me ache to be home.

I also started to understand a point I hadn't fully seen before.

I didn't want a life that was only about me.

But I also didn't want to lose myself inside a life that was only about everyone else.

I was trying to find a way to hold both.

Journal Entry — 2/12/24

Part of me thinks I should not go home until I have a plan. I still have more to learn here. But that means pushing myself further — getting out in the evenings, planning weekend activities, spending more time with colleagues.

It's not worth staying if I do not grow.
It's not time to coast.
It's time to live, learn, and make the most of this chapter... or go home.

If I go home, I want to feel like this chapter is complete. I don't want to wish days away. I want to learn about Alice, about myself, and about what I want from life.

But what would "complete" feel like?

Part of me wishes it were obvious—someone would wave a flag, a message would appear in the sky telling me, This is why you are here. This is what you're meant to learn. This is the path you're supposed to follow. Wouldn't that be nice?

But the whole purpose of this journey has been learning to listen to my inner voice. So why do I still expect clarity to arrive from a place outside of me?

Completion isn't a message I'll be told; it's a truth I'll feel. Maybe it's the moment I trust myself enough to know I've done the work I came here to do. Maybe that same gently voice I'm learning to hear now will be the one that tells me when it's time to go home.

I can't expect clarity to suddenly arrive.
I have to learn—again—to trust myself, be patient, and sit in the discomfort of not knowing.

Even when my mind is loud.
Even when the questions keep circling.

And in some way, the fact that I still need to remind myself of this is its own answer.

I'm not finished yet.

2/19/24 — ELLERY CREEK BIG HOLE

Camping at Ellery Creek gave me a glimpse of what balance might feel like.

Water is rare in the desert, which makes Ellery Creek feel almost sacred. Hidden between towering red cliffs, the water was cool, clear, and still—a quiet contrast to the harshness surrounding it.

Sliding into water felt like stepping into another world.

We floated, laughed, and brought ridiculous inflatables—including a giant whale—letting the heat of the day fade into softer moments. The simplicity of it all—the water, the cliffs, the sky—felt grounding in a way I hadn't lived.

Because of the heat, I couldn't burrow deep inside my swag the way I normally would when camping. Usually, I liked to tuck myself in tightly, zipped up like a cocoon—a small barrier between me and whatever creatures might be wandering around in the dark. But the warm night air meant I had to sleep mostly on top of the covers, which left me feeling oddly exposed.

I was still slightly on edge about snakes, carefully choosing a raised platform for my swag.

Still, I couldn't fully relax.

And yet, the night had its magic.

The stars stretched endlessly across the desert sky. We sat around the fire, sharing stories, sipping drinks, and snacking on cheese and crackers, which seemed to be a staple in my daily meals.

As the night grew quieter, I heard a sound I never heard before.

The distant call of dingos.

It echoed through the darkness—wild, haunting, and completely unforgettable.

This was why I had come.

Moments like this.
Moments that made me feel fully present. Fully alive.

And yet in that fullness, there was a quiet question underneath it all: How do I take this feeling home with me?

Because I knew I couldn't stay here forever.

But I also knew I couldn't go back unchanged.

THE PULSE OF THE TODD

As the weeks passed, my emotions came in waves.

Some days, I felt strong, clear, grounded.
Other days, I felt overwhelmed, emotional, unsure of everything.

At first, I thought I was the problem—I should be more stable, more certain, more decisive.

But over time, I began to understand it differently.

These feelings weren't problems.
They were signals.

They were asking me to slow down, listen, and pay attention to what mattered most.

I didn't need to have all the answers.
I needed to be willing to sit in the questions.

One of the most powerful moments came when I watched the Todd River flow.

Most of the year, the Todd is nothing more than a wide stretch of sand cutting through the center of town. People walk their dogs along it. Kids play in the dry riverbed. Cars cross it without a second thought. Beneath the shade of the tall river red gums, it hardly resembles a river at all.

The Todd is so famously dry the town celebrates it with humor. Every year, Alice Springs hosts the Henley-on-Todd Regatta—the only "dry river" boat race in the world. Competitors run down the sandy riverbed carrying boats with no bottoms while spectators cheer from the banks. Ironically, the race has occasionally been canceled for the most unusual reason possible—there was actually water in the river.

But when the rains come—often carried down from tropical storms and cyclones far to the north—everything changes.

At first, it doesn't look dramatic. There's no sudden wall of water. Instead, a thin ribbon of muddy water begins to wind its way through the sandy riverbed, carving a slow path forward. The front of the water moves surprisingly slowly, sometimes no faster than a walking pace. People gather along the banks, some walking beside it, watching as the desert river quietly comes back to life.

Gradually, the flow widens and deepens. The narrow stream grows into a moving ribbon of brown water stretching across the sandy channel. The soft desert soundscape shifts as the trickle becomes a steady rush moving through the heart of town.

Watching it unfold feels almost magical—like witnessing the desert slowly awaken after a long sleep.

Within hours, the landscape begins to change. The water replenishes underground aquifers, and dormant life responds almost immediately. Birds gather in surprising numbers, and the dry desert greens again.

Locals watch the weather closely during the rainy season, always asking the same hopeful question: *Do you think the Todd will flow?*

And when it does, people show up.

There's also a local legend: If you see the Todd River flow three times, you become a true local—and you'll never leave Alice Springs.

This was my second time seeing it flow.

And I couldn't help but wonder if there might be some truth to that.

This place gets into you.

The land, the vast spaces, the silence, the red dirt that clings to everything—it slowly seeps into your blood.

Standing there, watching the river come to life, I felt the shift.

Change doesn't happen all at once.

It happens slowly, beneath the surface, long before it's visible to anyone else.

Just like me.

BEAUTY, THEN FEAR

But in that moment of beauty, there was a feeling heavier underneath it.

A silent loneliness.

A tension I couldn't quite name.

For a while, I told myself it was homesickness.

But the more I sat with it, the more I understood that wasn't quite true.

This sadness wasn't homesickness.

It was fear.

Fear of where home really is.
Fear of missing whichever place I'm not in.
Fear of leaving here and longing to come back.
Fear of going home and feeling like I've outgrown parts of my old life.

Fear I might return and slip back into old patterns.
Or worse—I might return and still feel the same.

That was the part I hadn't expected.

It wasn't about choosing where to live.

It was about choosing who I would be in that life.

I knew leaving would be hard.

But going home would be hard too.

I could feel myself slowly preparing to return—to be a wife, a mother, a dog mom, a friend, a daughter. To step back into the life that had been waiting for me.

Another chapter was unfolding.

I wasn't sure I was ready to say goodbye to adventure.

And yet, I was starting to understand a shift I hadn't seen clearly before.

The magic didn't have to stay in Australia.

I could carry it with me.

The spaces of stillness. The sense of wonder. The connection to nature and to people. These weren't tied to a place—they were moments I could choose to create.

Camping trips with my family.

Swimming in hidden lakes
Mornings before the house wakes.
Evenings spent outside, noticing the sky.

Adventure doesn't end because geography changes.

It simply asks for intention.

Journal Entry — 2/20/24

The truth is, I'm still sorting through my emotions. I don't always understand why one day feels limitless and the next feels overwhelming. I may never have all the answers.

But I do have a more reflective understanding of myself—my needs, my patterns, my capacity for growth.

I know now staying present, listening to my heart, and honoring adventure and responsibility—is what makes life whole.

And that's where I stand now.

In progress.

Uncertain.

Learning.

Growing.

Still willing to embrace the unknown.

So, should I stay or should I go?

I don't have a clear answer.

But I know this: Australia has taught me how to be on my own. How to sit with uncertainty. How to choose growth, even when it's uncomfortable.

Home has taught me love. Connection. What it means to belong to a life beyond my own.

And the life I'm building—the person I'm becoming—isn't about choosing one over the other.

It's about learning how to carry both.

Because the truth is, I may leave the Outback.

But the part of me that learned how to feel alive here?

That part is coming with me.

CHAPTER 20:
THE GREAT OCEAN ROAD

Journal Entry — 4/9/24

I boarded the train to Geelong today with a mix of excitement and quiet self-awareness. I'm officially on holiday in Melbourne, headed toward the famous Great Ocean Road with my good mate, Amy — a journey I have dreamed about. I also cannot ignore the familiar, unwanted pull of my spending habits. I spent more than I should have, a reminder I'm still learning, still growing, still working through old patterns.

But this trip feels necessary.

More than a vacation, it feels like permission — permission to breathe, let go, think, feel, and sit with the big questions about what comes next in my life.

Melbourne itself was a whirlwind. We experienced four seasons in a single day, wandered through streets brimming with cafes and shops, and marveled at items we couldn't easily find in Alice Springs. It was indulgent and exhilarating, a prelude to the journey that awaited us along the coast.

The Great Ocean Road stretches roughly 150 miles along Victoria's southeastern coast. It's famous for dramatic cliffs, wild ocean views, and iconic landmarks like the Twelve Apostles. Even before seeing it, I can feel this journey will be about more than scenery. It feels like a step into greater understanding— a chance to reconnect with myself in a setting where land and sea meet in powerful ways.

Journal Entry — 4/11/24

The Great Ocean Road is nothing short of spectacular.

The roads wind along cliffs that drop dramatically into the ocean, offering breathtaking views of waves crashing against the rocks below.

One of our first stops was Teddy's Lookout, which offers spectacular views of the St. George River and the Great Ocean Road coastline.

Towering cliffs plunge into the ocean. Empty beaches stretch endlessly. The coastline seems to breathe with its own beat. Standing there, taking it all in, I felt small in the best possible way.

Our second day focused on the Twelve Apostles — the most famous section of the Great Ocean Road, featuring incredible rock formations carved by the Southern Ocean.

We walked down the Gibson Steps onto the beach for a close-up view of the rock formations. The perspective of the power of the waves and the height of the cliffs was unforgettable.

I learned this land holds powerful spiritual significance for Aboriginal people — connections to ancestors, wildlife, and the land itself. After seeing it with my own eyes, I understand. There's a presence here. A calm, grounding energy. Beauty like this doesn't exist without history, spirit, and stories woven into the land.

We drove through the lush rainforest of Port Campbell National Park and had the chance to see a koala in the wild — truly magical. I still feel the rush of excitement as I jumped out of the car to watch him.

Goosebumps covered my arms. My eyes filled with tears.

I stood completely still, completely present, watching him move slowly, turning his head side to side as if posing for me. It felt like our own private photo shoot. I could've stayed there for hours, soaking in every slow, gentle movement.

It was pure magic.

The road trip itself was filled with music and laughter. Amy was usually the DJ, and she introduced me to sea shanty songs — music I probably wouldn't have chosen on my own, but now I will always associate with her. Even if I only hear them intentionally, they will always bring me back to this time, to our laughs, to our conversations, and to our shared moments on the road.

We stopped at the bottle shop and bought lollies. I picked out my favorites, and Amy convinced me to try the tropical mix and the pineapple lumps, which became another small memory stitched into this trip.

Simple moments. Sweet moments. The kind I know I will treasure later.

This trip had all the good vibes of an Australian road trip: great music, lots of laughter, and unforgettable scenery. I am grateful for the chance to explore this beautiful part of Australia

Journal Entry — 4/22/24

The salt spray from the Southern Ocean clung to my skin as we wound our way out of Apollo Bay. Through the open window, the air carried a cocktail of brine and crushed eucalyptus. I leaned my head back against the seat, watching the rugged coastline blur into a line of turquoise and gold, and that's when it hit me—a shift in my chest.

The "knowing" didn't arrive with a shout; it was a steady, rhythmic pulse. **It's time.** I had been debating extending my contract until December, maybe longer, but the logic of "more time" suddenly felt hollow. I couldn't explain the reasons for you, but I felt them. My family needed me.

I looked over at Amy, the hum of the tires on the asphalt filling the silence between us. When I spoke the words aloud, she didn't offer a list of pros and cons. She leaned back, her eyes steady on the road ahead.

"If your instincts are telling you that," she said, her voice anchoring the moment, *"your decision is already made."*

Her calm settled over me like a gentle hand. The decision that had shadowed me for weeks melted away, replaced by a sudden, clear certainty.

The confirmation arrived the next day in the form of a ding from my phone. A text from Brooke carried a weight that traveled across oceans I could not ignore, so I called her on FaceTime. Her face lit up before she spoke, a mix of mischief and wonder.

"I'm pregnant," she said.

I gasped, laughter and tears mingling in my chest. **Grandma.** *I was going to be a grandma.*

"I wanted you to know first," she said. *I felt the unspoken meaning behind her words: This news was the sign I needed to come home. With Amy by my side, the three of us shared that moment through the screen, and the thousands of miles between Australia and home simply vanished.*

Then came the "impossible" request.

"You can't tell Dad," Brooke warned. *"I want to do it in person on Father's Day. I want to see his face."*

Keeping that secret felt like trying to keep an echo from escaping a canyon. My heart clenched with the weight of it. I wanted to stand on the red rocks of the Outback and scream it to the wind. I did end up whispering the news to a few friends in Australia—relying on the safety of a different hemisphere—but the guilt of Brad not knowing followed me like a shadow. Yet, the joy was simply too massive for one person to contain.

In an instant, my future looked different. I could see it all: the weight of a sleeping baby on my shoulder, miniature shoes by the door, and the feel of tiny, perfect fingers curled tightly around mine. Memories of my own children rushed back—reading **Sleeping Beauty** and watching **The 12 Dancing Princesses** a million times until I knew every word. Those moments were no longer only echoes of the past; they were a preview of what was to come.

I looked out at the vast Australian sky, feeling a sudden, profound surge of gratitude. I needed this red dirt. I needed to hear the call of the red-tailed black cockatoo and the sheer scale of the Outback to fill the empty spaces inside me. If this news had come a year earlier, I might never have stepped onto that plane. I had lived this adventure fully, breathed in air from this continent, and because I had, I could now go home without a single "what if."

I had listened to the voice that told me to go when my children were grown, and now I was listening to the voice telling me to return.

Before I left, I found a small shop and picked out a soft sleeper and a plush kangaroo with a tiny joey in its pouch. I wanted this baby to know, from the start, that they were connected to this part of my life. I wanted them to feel the spirit of the red earth and the wide-open skies in those gifts—and to know I had traveled across the world to be ready to hold their hand.

The universe whispers first, long before it ever shouts. The challenge isn't in finding the signs—it's in quieting myself enough to listen.

I'm trying to apply the same trust to my career.

I could have gone back to my old school position. It would have been safe. Established. Easy.

But my gut said no.

Not because it would be impossible — but because it would make me unhappy. And I know when I am unhappy, it affects others too.

My instincts tell me there are other opportunities waiting for me — even if I cannot see them yet.

I didn't get the position I recently hoped for, and I'm trying not to be heartbroken. Higher education positions will likely be difficult to find with funding shifts. Still, my inner voice is clear:

Do not return to the same teaching path.
Keep looking.
Keep believing.

I have applied for many positions. Some have sent polite rejections. Others have said nothing at all.

And yet, I feel a steady, subtle confidence at the depths of me.

A knowing.

The right opportunity is waiting. Patience is part of the lesson.

From the onset of this wild journey, I have followed my gut. And it has led me to kangaroos, friendships, breathtaking coastlines, and now back toward home.

For now, I plan to return home sometime between the end of June and September, depending on my family and when the right job appears.

What I do know is this: Australia has taught me to listen — not to the world around me, but to the gentle voice inside myself.

And that may be one of the greatest gifts this journey has given me.

The Great Ocean Road and the Twelve Apostles

CHAPTER 21:

THE UPS AND DOWNS OF THE OUTBACK

I struck a deal with Brolga: If I volunteered all day Saturday and Sunday, he would let me join him on set for the filming of *Kangaroo*. He laughed, agreed instantly, and we shook on it.

I was beyond excited.

What an incredible opportunity. It felt like this one year in Australia was packed with more once-in-a-lifetime experiences than most people get in decades.

I kept thinking, *How did I get so lucky?*

Journal Entry — 4/25/24

Today was an emotional roller coaster — soaring highs and vast lows.

I woke up excited about being on the set of the kangaroo movie while also feeling sad I would be saying goodbye to Penny tonight. Joy and heartbreak on the same day.

Penny made the hard decision that it was time for her to leave Alice after her house was broken into several times. A group of teenagers, fueled by a lack of fear that I couldn't fathom, began targeting her home. They came armed with wire cutters, slicing through the heavy metal security screens like they were paper before smashing the windows to force their way inside.

After a grueling, heart-heavy decision, Penny realized she couldn't stay. She decided to move far from the town, retreating into an extremely remote part of the Outback to live closer to her brother and family. In that deep desert, the rules of the world change. Crime there is settled in its own quiet, permanent way. You are gifted one warning, and if you make the mistake a second time, you simply disappear down one of the countless abandoned mine shafts.

One minute, I felt like crying. The next, I was staring at the clock, counting down the minutes until Brolga would pick me up and take me to the movie set.

Nervous. Thrilled. Sad. Grateful. All of it mixed like the perfect storm.

It was ANZAC Day. A day the country sets aside to remember the members of the Australian and New Zealand Army

Corps — the ANZACs — who served and died in wars, conflicts, and peacekeeping missions. Part of me wished I had gotten up early for the sunrise service. But I thought I would be filming all day. I also wanted to sleep in.

The extra time gave me space to clean, journal, and try to organize my life —a detail my heart clearly needed.

I told myself I would write after filming and again after dinner with Penny.

Life, of course, had other plans.

We didn't finish filming until after six p.m., and I needed to be at Penny's farewell dinner by then. So my journal entries had to merge into one, exactly as this day blended joy and sorrow into moments bittersweet and unforgettable.

I waited anxiously outside the gate, standing under a tree, watching for Brolga's car.

Since we had time before shooting began, he took me to see one of the cabins used in the film — the setting where the main character would live with the kangaroos.

Walking inside felt surreal. Every detail was carefully designed to look like a real, lived-in home.

What made it more meaningful was how closely it resembled the location Brolga lived when he first started the Kangaroo Sanctuary. It felt like art imitating life — reflecting what truly came from his heart.

I also got to see where special effects were being filmed.

One crew member had his hands and legs strapped together and was suspended on a large hoist. They lifted him into the air so he could jump like a kangaroo. These movements would later be transformed into special effects to recreate scenes of Roger chasing Brolga and asserting his dominance as alpha male.

Watching how they created these moments was fascinating. Seeing the mechanics behind the magic gave me a new appreciation for filmmaking. I kept thinking about how incredible it would be to see the final version on screen, knowing what went into making it.

When we arrived on set, the first order of business was lunch — and it was impressive.

So much food. So many choices. Incredible desserts.

I sat down at a table with Brolga without realizing I also sat right next to Ryan Corr. I honestly thought he was another bloke working on set. We chatted casually, and he was completely down-to-earth.

After he left, Brolga told me who he was.

I'm not familiar with Australian actors, so I hadn't realized I was sitting next to the star of the movie. I immediately wished I took a photo, but in a way, I'm glad I simply treated him like a normal person and enjoyed the moment for what it was.

Most of the day was spent waiting between scenes. I passed the time chatting with Brolga, trying not to overthink everything I said. I always worry I will say the wrong thing.

I didn't take many photos — partly because I didn't want to get in trouble and partly because I wanted to respect the opportunity. I also wanted to blend in and feel like I belonged rather than stand out as the awkward American outsider.

It was fascinating to watch the director review scenes on a large monitor, deciding whether they needed another take. The amount of equipment, the setup, the packing up, and moving everything a short distance to film again — it was a massive operation.

The filming took place not far from my donga, in a peaceful, tranquil part of the Outback.

RED-TAIL BLACK COCKATOO

A truly magical moment happened at the end of filming when the Outback reminded me where I was.

The first time I saw a red-tailed black cockatoo was the day we finished filming *Kangaroo*.

Before coming to Australia, I had only seen pictures of the bird and heard its call on television, but never in real life. I bought a lampshade painted with a red-tailed black cockatoo.

The excitement was slowly settling, the energy that had filled the air during filming fading into the quieter feeling that comes when meaningful events are ending. I knew the night ahead would carry the weight of goodbyes with Penny Fairweather, and my mind was already drifting toward that.

And then I heard it.

A call echoed across the sky.

When I looked up, several red-tailed black cockatoos were flying overhead. Their wings stretched wide against the bright blue sky, and the vivid bands of red beneath their tails caught the sunlight as they passed. They called again. It was impossible to ignore.

Seeing them overhead was one of the most beautiful sights I have ever witnessed and probably one of the most beautiful sights I ever will.

The feeling was like experiencing many of life's small, meaningful moments all at once — the first birds chirping in the morning, the call of an owl in the dark while sitting around a campfire, the smell of freshly cut grass, singing "Silent Night" on Christmas Eve, or the first sip of a pumpkin spice latte when the fall air finally turns cool. That's what the call of the red-tailed black cockatoo felt like to me.

In Indigenous Australian culture, the red-tailed black cockatoo carries spiritual meaning, though interpretations vary between communities. Some see it as a reminder to listen closely to intuition or as a signal that change is coming. At that moment, standing under the wide sky and watching them disappear across the horizon, I felt a personal connection. It was a quiet marker in time — a reminder of where I was, what I was experiencing, and how fully this area had begun to shape this chapter of my life.

It was a moment I waited for — a small, unexpected gift at the close of a full day. A pause before the evening, before the conversations, before the final waves.

THE NIGHT

As extraordinary as the day was, the night ended in heartbreak.

Tonight was Penny's farewell dinner.

Saying goodbye to her was far harder than I was prepared for.

There is a special pain in knowing you may never see someone again — someone who became such an essential part of your life in such a short time.

I am profoundly grateful to have met Penny. To have learned from her. To have loved her. To have been pushed by her.

She played a huge role in my success here and in helping me step far outside my comfort zone. She is full of spirit, spunk, and force of nature energy.

Penny Fairweather will always have a special place in my heart.

I think of her as a dear friend, but also as my Australian mum — the person I could go to for advice, tea, honesty, laughter, and reminders of why I am here.

It breaks my heart to know I won't be able to pop over and visit her anymore.

I understand why she's leaving. Alice Springs no longer feels safe for her. It's heartbreaking the area that feels safer is in the middle of the Outback, miles from almost everything and everyone.

That's a complex reality to understand.

I'm not ready to say goodbye — not to Penny, not to this place, not to this chapter of my life.

And yet, I know my time here is slowly coming to an end.

I have so much to look forward to: family, fresh starts, new chapters.

But I will carry an intense sadness about leaving this beautiful, complicated, soul-stirring place.

The Outback has taught me life is full of highs and lows — often in the same day.

It's a reminder to slow down. To savor laughter. To soak in moments with friends. To make memories while we can.

We are here to live life, not watch time pass.

I love you, Penny Fairweather.

Thank you for your wisdom, your advice, our many laughs, for being my personal tour guide, for pushing me far outside my comfort zone, and for being the absolute badass you are.

This place — and the people in it — have changed me forever.

CHAPTER 22:
THE FINKE DESERT RACE

From the day I arrived in Australia, everyone talked about the Finke Desert Race.

It came up in every conversation — part warning, part invitation.

When I first landed, Finke happened that weekend. Some people asked if I was going. Others laughed, as if to say, *Are you brave enough for that?*

Since I recently arrived, I decided it probably wasn't the best idea to dive straight into an experience so wild and intense. But I hoped someday, I would get the chance to see Finke for myself.

That time finally came.

This weekend was Finke, and I was going camping with Delsey and her family.

I felt nervous. Excited. Curious.

I heard so many mixed reviews, but I also knew this was a once-in-a-lifetime opportunity.

THE JOURNEY THERE

Getting there was an adventure in itself.

On the drive out, one of the trucks got a flat tire, so we pulled over to change it.

As we got closer, the landscape changed.

Hundreds of campsites lined the dusty roads, stretching across the red desert. This remote area, usually reserved and empty, came alive for one weekend each year — like a temporary city built on dust, motorbikes, and tradition.

Delsey and her friends had a regular camping spot, a spot they returned to year after year. Some people left campsites set up permanently, as if claiming their patch of desert — their own piece of Finke.

Eric and Delsey set up our area, their boys climbing into their tent above the ute.

I rolled out my swag, tossed in my pillow, blanket, and small duffel bag, and called it home.

Simple. Dusty. Perfect.

I cracked a beer and officially began the weekend.

We jumped in the car and drove around to check out other campsites. I was blown away by how many people were out there, living in all kinds of setups, all coming together for this one massive event.

It felt like the Outback version of a festival — but rougher, louder, and more real.

CAMPFIRE NIGHTS

That night, Delsey and her friends cooked dinner over the fire and made incredible cheese bread — the kind that tastes better when shared under an open sky. The smell drifted through the cool desert air, mixing with smoke and the faint sweetness of whatever others had cooking at their own campsites.

We drank, laughed, and told stories. The conversations were easy, unfiltered, and warm in a way that only happens when people gather around a fire.

Eric played music, and instantly, I was transported. The songs pulled me backward through time, stirring memories I hadn't realized I was still carrying.

One moment I was sitting in the Australian desert, and the next I was sixteen again, driving around in my little Geo Metro on a Saturday night with the windows down, feeling invincible. When **Dwight Yoakam's "Suspicious Minds"** came through the speakers, I could practically feel myself reaching over to rewind the cassette again and again to hear it one more time.

Then another song came on, and the feeling moved. **"It's Your Love" by Faith Hill and Tim McGraw** brought me straight back to my wedding day. My chest tightened with a mixture of love and longing. I missed my husband with a heavy, constant ache and wished he could be here beside me, experiencing this wild, beautiful moment in the middle of nowhere.

The **Kenny Rogers** songs carried me home. I could see Sunday nights clearly: the routine of carrying firewood into the house, the wood stacked neatly by the fireplace, the record player spinning in the same room we had filled with logs. Those songs brought the warmth of childhood, the comfort of home, and the simplicity of nights when everything felt steady and safe.

All around us, the desert pulsed with life. Campfires glowed in every direction; little pockets of light scattered across the dark. Music drifted from every angle — overlapping melodies, laughter, and conversations woven together in a warm, chaotic harmony. People moved freely from one campsite to the next, catching up with friends they only saw once a year, picking up conversations as if no time had passed.

The crowd was a mix of everything and everyone. One guy showed up in a full Stitch onesie, confidently stealing the karaoke mic whenever possible, singing lyrics he only half remembered with complete commitment. Others were bundled in beanies and layers, fighting the sharp chill of the desert night, while some wandered around in shorts and t-shirts like the cold didn't touch them at all.

The air smelled like smoke and grilled food. Fires cracked and popped. Laughter rose in waves. Conversations overlapped and carried through the night.

As I sat there, it became clear to me, I felt completely at ease. I never met most of these people before, yet there was no awkwardness, no pressure to impress or explain myself. People spoke openly, laughed freely, and accepted each other without hesitation. No one was trying to prove anything. Everyone was simply present.

That freedom — that acceptance — created an instant connection. It made strangers feel like old friends I've known forever.

I laughed until my stomach hurt. I breathed deeply.
I felt present.

And as I sat there surrounded by music, firelight, and people who felt like family despite being strangers only hours before, I knew this night would stay with me. Not because of any one moment, but because of how fully I felt everything — the music, the memories, the laughter, the belonging.

It was a moment I knew I would carry with me long after the fire burned out.

RACE DAY

The next morning, I woke up excited to see what Finke was all about.

We loaded up and drove closer to the track to watch the bikes and buggies fly past.

Watching the motorbikes fly over the hills was thrilling. I could hear helicopters overhead, picking up famous racers after each leg of the race and flying them back to prepare for the next run.

The Finke Desert Race is a legendary, two-day, multi-terrain off-road race held every year over the King's Birthday long weekend in the Northern Territory.

The race runs from Alice Springs to Finke and back, covering roughly 230 kilometers each way.

Bikes, cars, and buggies tear across red sand, dirt, and desert terrain at unbelievable speeds. Some bikes reach speeds of over 180 kilometers per hour.

It's considered one of the most difficult, dangerous, and fastest off-road races in the world.

For many locals, it's the best weekend of the year in Central Australia.

The atmosphere is electric.

Music pumps through the desert day and night. Thousands of people camp right beside the track, with tents, caravans, and wild setups only meters from the action.

It's dusty. Loud. Rowdy.

And somehow, completely perfect.

COMMUNITY IN THE DESERT

The crowd was a wild, come-one-come-all mix of people.

It felt like one giant community.

People wandered from campsite to campsite, sharing food, drinks, laughs, and stories. You could make friends in minutes.

Some of my favorite memories were the small, absurd, beautiful details.

Like learning how to dig a hole to use as a bathroom and realizing there is genuinely no "safe" private spot. At any moment, someone could come flying over a hill and see everything.

You laugh and adapt. Outback rules, I guess.

I also got a lesson on riding my first motorbike, which was both terrifying and awesome.

But my favorite moments were still the simplest — sitting around the campfire with drinks in hand, music playing, people singing, stories flowing, learning about this iconic Australian event that belongs on so many bucket lists.

AFTER THE WEEKEND

By the end of the weekend, everyone was covered in red dirt.

It took forever to wash it out of my hair. I had to shampoo multiple times to work through the layers of dust, and even then, it felt like the desert was still clinging to me.

I was exhausted. Sleeping in the swag — which is not exactly luxury — combined with music thumping through the night, spotlights sweeping across the dark, and a party that never really stopped meant sleep came in thin, broken stretches.

I'm grateful I had the chance to be part of Finke. I understand the hype around the event, and I also understand why it might not be for everyone. It is loud, dusty, and nonstop. Still, I'm grateful I got to be part of it. It showed me a side of the desert that's bold, communal, and alive in its own way.

And when you stop to consider the sheer number of volunteers, the planning, the coordination, the logistics behind it all, it becomes more impressive. What looks wild and untamed is actually carefully orchestrated.

GRATITUDE

I'm so grateful I got to experience Finke.

Additionally grateful Delsey brought me along with her family and let me be part of it — to see, hear, and feel it for myself.

She's a friend who makes you feel seen and included.

I only wish I had known her sooner. My time here is almost over, and it feels like I've begun to discover who she is — her strength, her generosity, and the heart she brings to everything she does.

I now know Finke isn't only a race.

It's red dirt that clings to your skin, engines roaring over hills, laughter echoing across the campsite, spotlights sweeping through the night, and the constant hum of activity. It's exhaustion and exhilaration; chaos and connection; a wild, unforgettable weekend that leaves its mark long after it's over.

CRUSTY
KNICKERS

10.06.2024

CHAPTER 23:
THE LAST FEW DAYS

Today is heavy with emotion. It's my last day at Larapinta. Writing that feels unreal.

This place has been a gift. Not always an easy one, but a gift all the same. Here, I've learned more than I expected — not merely about teaching, but about myself.

The past two weeks especially have stretched me. I've had to notice my own limits — when I'm tired, overwhelmed, running on empty.

I've learned I can't push through everything.
Sometimes strength looks like stepping back.
Sometimes it looks like being quiet.
Sometimes it looks like saying, I need a moment.

Teaching in Australia didn't introduce me to students — it introduced me to a different flow of the classroom.

The challenges weren't new, but the context was. The layers felt different. More complex. More tied to story and circumstance.

What changed in me wasn't my understanding of children — it was my understanding of myself inside the classroom.

I began to notice the classroom was a mirror; my students almost always reflected my own mood and reactions back to me. On the days when my tolerance was low and I responded with impatience, the students met me with that same friction. But on the days when I was able to respond instead of react — staying calm and grounded — the energy in the room shifted.

I remember one lesson when a student kept blurting out during instruction and pulling others off task. I could feel the disruption spreading, and my frustration building. My instinct was to shut it down quickly, firmly. Instead, I paused. Kept my voice steady. Redirected him without adding more heat to the room. I didn't match the disruption — I just held steady.

The energy settled, and the class came back without it escalating.

I learned it's hard to help regulate a dysregulated student if I'm not regulated myself. When I stayed calm, I became the steady point they could return to.

Here, patience had to last longer. Control mattered less than connection.

And now I understand why.

Structure and predictability matter. They create safety. They help students know what to expect. But control was never really about controlling behavior—because that's not **fully ours to have.**

What we do have is ourselves. Our tone. Our timing. Our reactions. Whether we pause or escalate.

The real control is in how we respond. And that response shapes what happens next — whether the behavior settles, spirals, or stays stuck.

It's not about forcing compliance. It's about creating enough safety that students can find their way back to regulation over time.

And that comes through connection.

Connection is knowing your students — their stories, their triggers, their strengths.
It's staying steady.
Noticing more than reacting.
Trying again the next day, even when the last one was hard.

Some days, progress isn't work completed. It's that we stayed steady with each other. A calmer voice. A slower response. Choosing not to escalate.

I see now how much of life sits in those small moments. Not big breakthroughs — just small choices made differently.

This lesson isn't only for the classroom. It's for me.

And I carry that with me as I return home — not as a teacher, but as a district behavior coach. This experience has changed how I think about supporting educators. Not because I have it all figured out, but because I understand more clearly where to begin.

I want to help create space for teachers to notice their own responses, to see the impact of tone and timing, and to understand connection as a starting point — not an extra piece.

It reminds me that growth rarely happens in big moments. It shows up in small ones: a pause, a softer tone, choosing not to react straight away.

Being here didn't change what I believe about students. It changed how I see myself inside the classroom — especially on the hard days, when patience runs thin.

I will miss so many people. I will miss so much about Alice Springs.

This journey changed me.

But I'm ready to go home.

I came here to stretch myself. To see differently. To live differently.

I did that.

And I'm leaving with a clearer sense of what I can control, what I can't, and where my energy actually belongs. Not with all the answers —only a better starting point.

PARRTJIMA

Parrtjima is one of the reasons I fell in love with Alice Springs.

Every year, the festival transforms the desert into an event I still don't have the right word for. Color and story layered across the red earth, the MacDonnell Ranges sitting quiet behind all of it. The Arrernte word *Parrtjima* — pronounced par-chee-ma — means to shine a light on something, in both the physical and enlightenment sense.

This year's theme was interconnectedness across Indigenous cultures. You could feel it without being told — in the installations, the crowd, the stories carried through light and sound and music.

The moment I keep coming back to is the puppet. Large-scale, slow-moving, the puppet was mesmerizing to watch as she walked through the crowd, sharing language and stories We didn't only watch — we followed, quiet and close, pulled along without quite deciding to be.

My favorite installation was the paintings brought to life through animation — art that shifted and moved and told its story in layers. And then the red-tailed black cockatoos called out overhead. Sharp, unmistakable. That sound didn't below to the festival; it belonged to the desert.

I love those cockatoos almost as much as I love my kangaroos. Their sound is tied to this setting in a way I've stopped trying to explain. Which is probably why, standing there in the glow of the lights, I felt the thing I'd been quietly avoiding — I was running out of nights like this one.

When I leave, I won't see them again. Not like this. Not here.

So I stood a little longer. Watched the light move across the desert. Listened for the cockatoos. Let the puppet disappear into the crowd. You can't take a kangaroo home. But maybe you can take the memory of standing in the dark in the middle of the Australian desert, watching painted stories move across a mountain, with cockatoos calling somewhere above you in the dark.

I'm trying to take that with me.

Journal Entry — 6/28/24

Today, I'm sitting at Emily and Jessie Gaps, trying to soak in the peace, the stillness, and the beauty.

I only have a couple of days left before I leave, and I may never see this land again.

That thought feels heavy.

I wish I slowed down more. I wish I allowed myself more moments like this — sitting, breathing, letting the land speak without trying to capture or accomplish anything.

Maybe that's the final lesson.

Not everything meaningful has to be achieved.
Some moments just have to be felt.

I have mixed emotions about going home.

I have anxiety about flying — the long journey, the fear of lost luggage, the endless hours in the air.

But there's also pride.

So much pride.

I did this.

I came to the other side of the world. I faced fears I didn't know I carried. I proved to myself I'm stronger and braver than I ever imagined.

I don't want to lose the teachings I learned here.

I don't want to fall back into old habits — numbing out on my phone, shopping when I feel overwhelmed, or using food for comfort instead of hearing what I truly need.

I learned when I feel overwhelmed, I need nature. I need movement. I need connection with something real.

Not scrolling. Not spending. Not hiding.

Purely living.

I am beyond brave.

I can face fear.

I can trust my gut.

I can believe in myself.

I need to slow down and listen to myself, rather than letting fear or pride decide for me.

Coming home will bring challenges. But coming to Australia brought challenges too — and I handled them.

I will handle what comes next as well.

This time, I will have my husband, my kids, my family, and my friends close by.

I hope I can inspire them to dream big, follow their hearts, take risks, and live fully.

I'm not on this earth to please others, impress others, chase likes on social media, or collect false friendships.

I'm here to lead with kindness, love deeply, and leave every place a little better than I found it.

Today feels like a sacred ending.

We had a kangaroo release, and I finished my final shift at the Kangaroo Sanctuary.

A kangaroo release is magical and incredibly intense.

We wait inside while Brolga brings one kangaroo at a time into the small yard. He places them gently into sacks and brings them inside.

Two of us secure the top of each bag with zip ties while someone sits nearby, keeping the kangaroos calm and talking softly to them.

When Brolga is outside, there is no talking. Absolute silence.

Every movement matters. Every sound matters.

The tension is thick because all we want is for the kangaroos to be safe and stress-free.

Once all the kangaroos are secured, we load them into trucks and drive out bush to release them.

We line the sacks up, cut the zip ties, and watch.

Some kangaroos hesitate. Some look back, as if asking, **Is it really time?**

Some hop a little, stop and look again.

Others leap out without hesitation — ready for freedom.

People often ask if I cry during releases.

I do.

But it's a complicated kind of crying.

You raise these joeys from when they're tiny. You feed them. Hold them. Protect them. Worry about them.

And one day, you set them free — knowing you may never see them again.

There is sadness. Fear for what might happen to them.

But also heartfelt gratitude.

I was part of their story. I helped them return to where they belong.

We always release joeys with a buddy they were raised with.

Watching two joeys hop off together into the bush is one of the most peaceful, beautiful things in nature I have ever seen.

It feels like love.

It feels like hope.

As I finished my final shift at the sanctuary, I felt all those emotions at once.

I held each kangaroo one last time and cried.

Knowing my time here had ended.

Knowing my time in the Red Centre was over.

Knowing I may never care for kangaroos like this again.

But also knowing it was time to go home.

I miss my family.

I miss my friends.

And most of all, I'm ready to be a grandmother.

Brolga came by to check on the kangaroos. I could tell he knew I had been crying. He kept the visit short, which I appreciated.

I didn't want to cry in front of him.

He said goodbye and told me to come back and visit.

I told him I plan to.

And like that, my time at the Kangaroo Sanctuary came to an end.

Not with a bang.

But with full hearts, gentle tears, and a primal understanding this extraordinary, life-changing chapter was complete.

Journal Entry — 6/30/24

I have embraced a small, dusty town in the middle of Australia.

Now it's time to say my farewells.

Leaving home for a new place was challenging. But saying goodbye to the place that became my second home feels even harder.

I'm grateful I followed my heart and chose to teach in Australia.

Connecting with different cultures and meeting new people have been profoundly rewarding. It enriched my life in ways I never imagined.

I am leaving here richer in memory and deeper in understanding.

This adventure taught me to cherish simple moments, value genuine connections, and embrace the beauty of nature in our diverse world.

I'm grateful for the opportunities and the incredible people who made this year unforgettable.

They have promised to visit — and I will hold them to it.

Here's to the next chapter of life and the people and experiences that truly matter.

I love you, Australia.

CHAPTER 24

THE GOODBYES THAT CHANGED ME

There's a particular heartbreak that comes not from loss, but from choice.

The hardest part of Australia wasn't the heat, the fear of snakes, or the isolation.

It was the leaving.

Suitcases open on the bed feel innocent at first. You fold clothes. You check lists. You weigh bags.

But beneath the surface of preparation rests heavier thoughts—the unspoken awareness that you're about to step away from routine, comfort, and everything familiar yet again, but in a different setting and context.

Airports have become sacred locations in my life.

They are thresholds.

Between who I was and who I am becoming.

LEAVING MY GIRLS

There is no strength in pretending it doesn't hurt.

When I said goodbye to my daughters before I left, I felt pulled in two directions. One part of me wanted to stay rooted exactly where I was. The other part knew I needed to go.

Choosing to leave —only temporarily — felt like betrayal and bravery tangled together.

I wondered:

Will they understand?
Will they resent me?
Am I choosing myself over them?

The truth is complicated.

What I know now is this: I wasn't choosing something over them. I was choosing something for myself.

I was choosing growth. I was choosing to step beyond what was comfortable. I was choosing to show them life does not shrink at a certain age — and you don't have to follow the expected path simply because it feels safe.

But knowing that does not make goodbye easier.

You hug a little longer.

You try not to cry.

You walk away because if you don't, you might not go at all.

That's the truth.

LEAVING BRAD

Leaving Brad was heavy in a quieter way.

When someone you love looks at you — really looks at you — and you know your choice affects them too, the weight settles far down in your chest.

There's no dramatic speech. No goodbye like you see in the movies. Only two people standing there in the in-between, knowing this is hard.

The silence between us held a shared understanding. I wasn't choosing a path away from him; I was choosing the path that lived inside me.

Still, when you walk toward security and turn around one last time, and the person you love is standing on the other side of the gate — growing smaller with each step — your chest cracks open.

No one talks about how brave it is to keep walking.

LEAVING WHO I WAS

Every goodbye also meant letting go of an older version of myself.

The version who stayed because it was easier.

The version who worried too much about what everyone else thought.

The version who talked herself out of possibilities before she tried.

Leaving forced me to look at my life honestly.

If I stayed, I know myself. I would have slipped back into old habits. I would have felt stuck. I would have felt disappointed for not going.

Going doesn't solve everything.

But it keeps me moving forward.

And sometimes movement is the difference between existing and living.

WHAT GOODBYES TEACH YOU

Goodbyes show you what matters.

They remind you who you love.

They reveal what you're afraid of and afraid of losing.

They force you to decide what life you want.

I used to think leaving meant choosing one life over another.

Now I understand sometimes leaving is how you honor both.

Leaving doesn't mean abandoning one life to embrace another. It means holding both in your heart at once — the life you are stepping away from and the life you are stepping toward. It's recognizing love isn't possession, and connection doesn't depend on constant presence. Leaving can be an act of respect — for the people you love, for yourself, and for the life you are called to live.

Honoring means acknowledging love and responsibility can exist alongside ambition and curiosity. It means allowing yourself to move without guilt, while carrying the people and experiences you cherish in your heart. It's a delicate balance, but it's also a profound gift — for yourself and for everyone you leave behind.

Because the woman who steps onto the plane returns changed — and she brings growth back with her.

Strength.
Perspective.
A deeper capacity for gratitude.

The goodbyes changed me because they forced me to ask:

Who am I when I choose growth over comfort?
Who am I when I allow my life to expand beyond what feels safe?

I learned I can love my family fiercely and still leave.

I can miss people and still move forward.

I can feel guilt and excitement at the same time.

That's not weakness.

That's being human.

CHAPTER 25:
RETURNING HOME

I didn't write much in my journal when I first returned home. Not because I didn't feel anything — but because I felt too much.

The transition was harder than I expected.

As excited as I was to be home, part of my heart was still in Australia.

It felt good to sleep in my own bed again. To hug my family. To sit in my favorite chair. To hear familiar voices.

But I also missed my home in Australia.

I missed my friends.

I missed my students.

I missed my kangaroos.

I found myself thinking about the smallest moments — the walk around the school at the end of the day, locking up the gates with Mullins and the crew. Friday nights with a beer and chips. The drive from my donga through the gap each morning. The song that played at the start of the school day. The mountains rising beyond the playground. The endless blue sky.

I didn't simply miss a place.

I missed a version of myself that existed there.

Reverse culture shock is real.

No one really prepares you for how strange your own life can feel when you return. You know where everything is — the grocery store, the streets, the routines — but somehow, it all feels slightly out of place. You speak the language, recognize the faces, and understand the culture, yet a part of you has shifted. It's the unsettling feeling of being home but not quite fitting into the pace the same way you once did.

Part of it is your life changed while everyone else's stayed mostly the same.

You return with experiences that shaped you in ways that are difficult to explain. When people ask, "How was it?" they're usually looking for a quick answer. But the truth is, there isn't a quick answer. What you carry with you feels more like a soul full of moments, wisdom carved by time, and lessons that can't be summarized in a few sentences.

It can make you feel strangely lonely, even in a room full of people.

I also noticed aspects of home I never paid attention to before. After living in the reserved simplicity of the Outback, the abundance here felt overwhelming.

Grocery shopping became exhausting. Too many options. Too many people. Too many decisions.

I didn't like the crowds. I didn't like the endless aisles. I didn't like the pressure of choosing.

In Australia, life felt simpler.

Fewer choices. Less stuff. Less stress.

Here, I had everything — and somehow felt more overwhelmed.

I missed the Australian accent. I missed hearing different languages on the street. I missed the cultural diversity. I missed waking up not knowing exactly what the day would hold.

Here everything was predictable.

And somehow, after the wide-open uncertainty of the desert, that predictability felt strangely unsettling.

Slowly, I came to know discomfort wasn't what needed to be fixed. It was simply the space between who I was before Australia and who I became while I was there. The desert had changed the way I saw life. It had taught me to slow down, to notice more, to live with less. Coming home didn't erase those truths. It meant learning how to carry them with me in a place that once felt completely identifiable.

SOMEWHERE IN THE MIDDLE

Coming home to the same school district I had taught in for twenty years, but this time in a new role as the district behavior coach wasn't what I expected either.

Everything looked familiar: the systems, the schedules, the routines, but I didn't return with some life-changing realization or a perfect plan to fix education in the United States. I didn't come back with answers. What I brought back was perspective.

And hopefully, that's what makes this new role meaningful.

I'm excited to work alongside teachers at all grade levels, not because I have everything figured out, but because I don't. I still have so much to learn, areas where I want to grow, and questions I'm still asking. But I also carry perspectives that might help others see things differently too.

My time teaching in the Northern Territory gave me a different way of seeing schools, students, and behavior. I know my views reflect just one part of Australia, but the differences were clear.

In Australia, there are fewer formal systems. There's more reliance on teacher judgment, relationships, and restorative practices. Students are given more independence, and teachers have more autonomy. Learning often feels flexible—focused on creating, exploring, and building, with more time for play and well-being.

But what stood out to me is there was still consistency.

Expectations were clear, and I never felt like students fell through the cracks or didn't get the support they needed. The difference wasn't in whether support existed—it was in how it happened. The processes felt less rigid, less formal, and didn't require constant reporting or documentation to the same extent as in the United States.

In Iowa, the approach is different. Schools rely heavily on systems—data, structure, standardization, and accountability. There are clear frameworks for identifying and supporting students, along with access to specialists like counselors, psychologists, behavior interventionists, and social workers. The days are structured, fast-paced, and focused on academic achievement.

I felt that difference immediately.

The schedules here are tight, planned down to the minute. Schools are built on bell-to-bell instruction. It's efficient but exhausting for both students and teachers. There's a constant movement from one thing to the next, with little downtime for students. It can feel like a rush from the moment they arrive until the moment they leave.

I'm not suggesting teachers here don't pause, don't listen, or don't create space for students to share meaningful parts of their lives. They do.

But after teaching in Iowa for over twenty years, I know what that pressure feels like.

The constant awareness of time.

The stress of making sure you're not falling behind in the curriculum.

The quiet decisions to set aside meaningful tasks so you can get through what feels necessary.

That pressure is real—and it's strong.

It's a feeling I still carry, and one I still see in teachers now that I've returned from Australia.

And yet, I also see the value in what exists here.

There are supports in place that simply didn't exist where I was teaching in Australia. Systems, while not perfect, provide consistency and help ensure students don't fall through the cracks.

That's why I can't say one way is better than the other.

I live somewhere in the middle now.

In Iowa, school often feels like a place you go to work—focused, structured, goal-oriented. In the Northern Territory, it felt more like a place you go to belong—where relationships and community came first.

What I carry with me now is the balance between those two ideas.

I still work within a system built on achievement, but I try to bring in moments of belonging. It's the pause in a busy day. The time spent listening to a student's story. The understanding that sometimes the work can wait when the human in front of you needs more.

In Iowa, success is often seen as a climb—higher scores, higher goals. In the Northern Territory, it felt more like a circle—connection, shared moments, and community.

Every classroom I step into carries a little bit of both worlds—the one I came from and the one that changed me.

That's the compass I carry now.

Not a force that points me in one fixed direction, but a reminder to keep adjusting, keep learning, and keep noticing.

Journal Entry — 7/2/25

It's hard to believe it has been a full year since I came home.

A year since I've seen the red dirt. Hugged my friends. Cared for a kangaroo. Heard Aussie slang that made me tilt my head in confusion.

In 365 days, I've realized an important truth.

Australia will always live in me.

Adventure changes you.

But so does coming home.

I'm not the same person I was before I left.

And I don't want to be.

I've grown in ways that are hard to measure but impossible to ignore.

I see the world differently now.

I notice excess.

I question busyness.

I crave simplicity.

I have become more certain about what matters — and less tolerant of what doesn't.

Growth means seeing more clearly.

It means standing up for what truly matters, even when it makes others uncomfortable.

It means choosing depth over distraction.

Australia gave me stories I will tell for the rest of my life.

It gave me resilience.
It gave me courage.
It gave me perspective.
It reminded me fewer choices and less stuff really do equal less stress.

But most of all, it gave me proof.

Proof I can do what scares me.
Proof discomfort isn't made to run from.
Proof growth lives outside the edges of what feels safe.

It taught me the voice buried within me—the one that whispers, Go—is worth paying attention to. Even when it's inconvenient. Even when it's scary. Even when it doesn't make sense to anyone else.

Living outside my comfort zone didn't break me.
It strengthened me.

And now, at home again, I don't need to recreate Australia to carry what it gave me.
I need to keep saying yes to the gentle inner nudge that asks for more.
That's the real gift.

And that is a lesson I will never unlearn.

WISHES TO MY FUTURE SELF

Dear future me,

When life becomes loud again, remember the silence of the desert.

When you feel yourself shrinking to fit expectations, remember how vast the sky felt — and how naturally you belonged beneath it.

When fear tells you to choose safety over calling, remember you once crossed oceans with nothing but faith and a suitcase.

Don't forget the woman who learned to breathe again in the Red Centre.

Keep choosing courage over comfort.

Keep choosing wonder over routine.

Keep choosing depth over distraction.

And if you ever feel lost, close your eyes.

Picture the red earth.

Feel the heat.

Hear the call of the red-tailed black cockatoos overhead.

Remember who you became there.

You are braver than you know.

You always were.

THE DESERT IS CALLING AGAIN

The first time I came to the desert, I was searching—though at the time, I couldn't have told you exactly what for. A part of me beneath the surface simply knew I needed to go. I followed that subtle pull all the way to the red earth surrounding Alice Springs, trusting a feeling that made more sense in my heart than it did in my head.

This time feels different.

I'm not coming back to find something new.
I'm coming back to listen again.

To the stillness of early mornings and the glow of sunsets that linger just a little longer than expected.

And to the things my heart already knows it's missed.

I can't wait to see a kangaroo again.

I know I'll make my way back to the sanctuary, hoping—maybe even a little bit expecting—to see some of the ones I cared for when they were small. Disco Dave and Beyoncé. The thought of seeing them again, grown but still there, feels like reconnecting with a piece of my own story.

I look forward to throwing my swag out on the red dirt, falling asleep under a blanket of stars, and waking to the sound of birds welcoming the morning as the sun rises over the desert.

I hope to hear the deep, steady drumbeat of an emu in the distance at night, and I wish for the chance to hear the unmistakable, almost magical call of the red-tailed black cockatoo echoing through the air.

I'm looking forward to seeing the people who made Alice feel like home, and to returning to the school where I once spent my days teaching—this time simply to give back, to volunteer, and to reconnect.

Part of me hopes to see the Todd River flowing while I'm there—**a rare, special sight**—but I know that isn't mine to control.

In the summer of 2026, I will return to Australia for eight weeks. The truth is, I don't have much of a plan. There's no carefully mapped itinerary waiting, no long list of reservations or destinations I must reach. I don't know exactly where I'll stay, who I will see, how I'll get around, or what my days will hold.

And strangely, that feels right.

Sometimes the best plan is not having one at all—learning to trust events will unfold the way they're meant to. There's a tranquil freedom in that faith. It asks you to let go of control and believe the path will appear when it needs to.

I have a ticket there and a ticket home. Even those could change if they needed to. The only thing I know for certain is that I'm going.

What I'm most excited about is the journey across the Outback with Penny Fairweather, which will be my first stop. This part of the journey—thankfully—is in more than capable hands. She has planned a week-long drive across the desert with the kind of precision that only someone who truly understands the Outback can manage. Traveling with Penny feels like stepping into both an adventure and a lesson.

She once shared with me that growing up, she changed primary schools fifteen times—moving between homes and people. And with time, she came to understand what that gave her.

"It made me absorb many different ways of being and thinking," she said. "It made me eager to expand. It also gave me a love of change—people, places, work.

"It taught me about judgment and how controlling that can be. If you judge someone, it becomes an excuse not to learn from them or see them differently.

"And if I react negatively to someone, I remind myself to walk in their shoes.

"We all have our own paths to maturity. We don't always realize how much our experiences shape us.

"And I've never forgotten that I am a warrior—as I believe most women are. It helps me speak up against unkindness, unfair behavior, and cruelty."

Those words stay with me.

Especially as we head into the vastness of the Outback—where plans matter, but mindset might matter still more.

She's already agreed we'll stop for every kangaroo we see along the side of the road, checking each pouch for a joey—just in case. She's packing bottles and formula alongside all the gear needed for such a remote trip, preparing for the possibility we might be able to help.

And maybe, just maybe, we will.

Maybe I'll get the chance to rescue a joey, to care for it, to nurture it—as I once did—and return it to the Kangaroo Sanctuary to continue its journey until it's ready to go back to the wild.

We will begin in Andamooka and travel north across vast stretches of country, following remote four-wheel-drive tracks through areas like Hawker, Willow Springs Station, and the opal-mining town of Coober Pedy.

From there, we'll make our way to Oodnadatta and follow the legendary Oodnadatta Track, continuing through Mount Dare and Old Andado Station before in the end arriving in Alice Springs.

Penny has the entire route mapped out—down to the miles we will drive each day and the isolated spots where we can stop for food or fuel. Out there, in the middle of the Outback, that kind of planning matters. Distances are vast, services are few, and the land demands respect.

So, I am happily leaving those details in her hands.

But once we reach Alice Springs, the plan dissolves again.

And I find myself back where I began—open to whatever the desert has waiting for me.

Of course, a small voice in my head tells me I should plan more. It whispers its worries in soft moments, reminding me of recent events and circumstances far beyond my control have left me feeling uncertain at times. Traveling across the world can feel like a bold choice when so much in life—and in the world—seems unpredictable. But still with that uncertainty, the pull to go remains stronger than the doubt.

I have felt this call before. I know what it sounds like.

It isn't loud. It doesn't demand attention. It simply waits patiently until you're ready to listen.

And this time, I am.

Perhaps the summer of 2026 will become the next chapter of this story. Maybe it will be the opening of part two. Or maybe it will simply be another restful season in the desert where I once again learn to slow down, pay attention, and trust the path unfolding in front of me.

Whatever it becomes, I know this much.

The desert is calling again.

And I am going to follow.

EPILOGUE

WHAT THE DESERT TAUGHT ME

When I first stepped onto Australian soil, I thought I was chasing adventure.

I didn't realize I was searching for myself.

Australia didn't offer comfort. It offered space.

And in that space, there was nowhere to hide.

The desert taught me silence isn't empty. It's revealing.

Out there — surrounded by red dirt and endless sky — distraction fell away. There were no packed schedules to hide behind. No noise loud enough to drown out my own thoughts.

I had to slow down.

I had to listen.

I had to face the parts of myself I had been avoiding.

Adventure rarely looks the way it does in photographs.

Yes, there were sunsets that stole my breath. Kangaroos bounding across open land. Skies so wide they made me feel small in the best possible way.

But there was also homesickness.

Missed birthdays.

Hard goodbyes.

The ache of loving people from far away.

I learned joy and ache can exist in the same breath.

That growth is uncomfortable.

That the longer, harder road is often the one that changes you most.

While I was there, I kept thinking about the song "A Thousand Miles from Nowhere" by Dwight Yoakam — *"I'm a thousand miles from nowhere. There's no place I'd rather be."*

That's exactly how it felt.

I was far from everything familiar — and exactly where I needed to be.

The desert stripped away excess.

It taught me less truly can be more.

That happiness isn't found in adding more noise, more possessions, more validation — but sometimes in removing what doesn't matter.

It taught me assumptions build walls, but curiosity builds connection.

That respect isn't optional — it's foundational.

That confidence is quiet.

That insecurity is loud.

It reminded me to look up at the sunrise instead of down at my phone.

To listen to understand, not to respond.

To make the moment right instead of waiting for the right moment.

It taught me the most important relationship I will ever have is the one I have with myself.

And if you really want to test yourself, go to an unknown place that stretches you — for me, that was the Outback.

The desert didn't fix me.

But it cleared the clutter.

It reminded me of who I am without distraction.

It showed me I'm capable of more than I once believed — and I don't have to live small simply because it feels safe.

I went looking for adventure.

I came home knowing myself better.

And that has made all the difference.

ACKNOWLEDGMENTS:
THE PEOPLE AND PLACES THAT HELD ME

TO LARAPINTA PRIMARY SCHOOL

To everyone at Larapinta Primary School,

Thank you for taking a chance on a slightly crazy American woman in the middle of a midlife adventure.

You didn't have to say yes to me. I came with an accent, big feelings, a suitcase full of uncertainty, and a heart that was both brave and breaking.

But you opened your doors anyway.

Thank you for trusting me.
For teaching me.
For guiding me through systems and routines so different from what I had known.

Thank you for being gentle on the days I quietly missed home. You never made me feel foolish for the tears that caught me off guard. You noticed. You checked in. You encouraged me without making it heavy.

And thank you for teaching me what not to do when I see a snake. (Apparently, screaming "run for your life" is not the recommended response.)

You welcomed me as more than a colleague. You treated me like family.

You looked after me. You made sure I was safe, included, and learning — not only professionally, but culturally.

You put up with my sarcasm.
My strange humor.
My constant need for translation.

Because of you, I didn't work in the Outback — I experienced it.

In a place between classrooms and dusty car parks, something inside me came back to life.

You gave me purpose again.

You reminded me midlife is not a winding down. It can be an awakening.

I will forever be grateful.

TO THE KANGAROO SANCTUARY

To Tahnee and Brolga,

Thank you for giving me a chance.

Even after all the messages.
Even after I probably made you question my sanity.
Even after I showed up with more enthusiasm than experience.

You trusted me with your joeys.

That's not a responsibility I take lightly.

Every weekend, driving through red dust toward the sanctuary, I felt the privilege of being invited into the sacred. Warming bottles. Tucking joeys into pouches. Learning their pulse of the red earth.

And Beatrice.

Watching her grow, laughing at the force with which she attacked her bottle — it was impossible not to fall in love with her spirit. She reminded me how much joy lives in simple moments.

Thank you for letting me see the work behind the scenes on the movie set. It made me feel included. It made the experience bigger and more real than I imagined.

Thank you for letting me witness the releases.

There are few moments in life more beautiful than watching a kangaroo hesitate for a breath — then bound into open land and freedom.

Standing there, knowing I had been a small part of that journey, is a memory I will carry for the rest of my life.

You didn't let me visit.

You let me belong.

TO PENNY FAIRWEATHER

Penny,

You didn't welcome me to the desert.

You welcomed me to your home.

You showed me how to make pumpkin pie the right way — patiently, properly, without shortcuts.

More importantly, you refused to let me skim the surface of Australia.

On the days I missed my girls.
On the days the ache of distance felt heavy.
You nudged me out the door.

"There's more to see," you'd say.

And there always was.

You modeled a life that doesn't shrink with age — it expands. It risks. It laughs loudly. It books the ticket.

Because of you, I stopped acting like my best chapters might already be written.

You didn't show me Alice Springs.

You showed me possibility.

TO MY SISTER AND BROTHER-IN-LAW, JIM AND MELISSA WILLIAMS —

Thank you for loving our dogs while Brad traveled to visit me — especially when Birdie was sick. It still makes me smile that Melissa claims she "doesn't like dogs," yet Birdie somehow ended up with new toys, extra snuggles, and what appeared to be a full spa retreat in your bed.

Knowing Birdie was spoiled and cared for allowed Brad and me to fully enjoy our time together so far from home.

AND TO MY NEPHEWS — CALEB AND TYLER WILLIAMS —

Thank you for babysitting Uncle Buck while mean Aunt Becky was away. Keeping him busy on the golf course and entertaining him with your constant humor was no easy task, and I'm grateful he had such good company.

TO THE PEOPLE OF ALICE SPRINGS —

Thank you for sharing your space and allowing me to experience the tranquil magic of the Outback desert.

This community is far more than red dirt and wide horizons.

It's alive with gatherings, markets, and constant opportunities to get involved, learn, and grow.

You welcomed me into that harmony.

The desert gave me space to breathe and to notice life without constant distraction.

But it was the people who made that space feel warm rather than lonely.

Your kindness, patience, and guidance helped Alice feel like home, although I deeply missed my family in America.

The red earth and wide-open skies will always hold a sacred spot in my heart.

The Outback taught me there may be no better classroom for resilience than this landscape — raw, honest, and expansive. It stretches you if you let it.

I'm especially grateful for the everyday connections — from Alan at Stuart Highway Autos, who kept me safely on the road, to the comfort of coffee and conversation at Yaye's Café, my favorite stop in town.

I look forward to returning in June of 2026 — to stand again on red dirt, breathe in dry air, and continue the growth that began there.

TO MY PARENTS, DAVE AND WANDA VOLL —

Thank you for your reassurance, although it might have been easier to tell me I was crazy for going.

Thank you for giving me a childhood rooted in imagination — building forts in the backyard, running through cornstalks, playing outside until the light faded. I'm grateful my days were shaped by fresh air instead of a television screen. Those early adventures taught me creativity and was the foundation that carried me all the way to Australia.

TO MY SISTERS, JILL WOLKEN AND BETH DENSON —

Thank you for listening to my endless voice memos and text messages about kangaroos and whatever new obsession captured my attention that week. You never made me feel like I was too much.

More importantly, thank you for taking such good care of Mom and Dad while I was away. Knowing they were surrounded by your steady love and care allowed me to fully step into this experience without fear. That peace of mind was a gift I can never repay.

TO MY HUSBAND, BRAD KNUDSON —

Thank you for believing in me and understanding this adventure wasn't about leaving, but about growth. It would've been easier to question it or ask me to stay. Instead, you told me to go because you know me.

You loved me from afar, answered the middle-of-the-night calls when I was homesick, and talked me through the moments I wanted to quit. When I begged you to book me a flight home, you reminded me why I went.

Thank you for holding down our world while I was away. I'm especially grateful I returned to find it all still standing and mostly in one piece. That alone deserves recognition.

Distance didn't weaken us. If anything, it clarified us. It reminded me partnership isn't about holding each other back — it's about standing steady while the other stretches.

Most of all, thank you for the gift of trust. Not control. Not permission. Trust.

That may have been the bravest thing of all.

TO MY GIRLS — AND TO MELROSE —

To my girls,

If I ever made you feel like I was choosing a place over you, please know this: I was choosing growth.

Loving you never shrank when I crossed an ocean.

It stretched.

I hope you always remember we're allowed to evolve. We're allowed to dream. We're allowed to step into new — at any age.

And to my granddaughter, Melrose — and to any grandchildren who may come after —

I hope you grow up knowing:

Adventure is not irresponsible.
Loving completely sometimes requires brave farewells.
The world is much bigger than most people explore.

Many visitors take a photo at the Sydney Opera House and say they've seen Australia. I only ever saw that city from an airport window.

The Australia that changed me lives in the red center. In dry riverbeds. In gum trees gripping the earth with stubborn resilience.

I hope your life is that bold. That untamed. That honest.

Don't follow the path of others.

Make your own — and walk it bravely.

True joy comes from loving yourself, following your heart, and building a life that feels like your own.

A DAY AT THE
KANGAROO SANCTUARY

Because the sanctuary was such a massive part of my experience, I wanted to capture what a typical day there really looked like—the pace, the work, and the peaceful magic of caring for the kangaroos.

Before I completely step into a "typical day," it's hard to fully understand the sanctuary without understanding the reality kangaroos face in the Outback.

In many ways, kangaroos reminded me of deer back in Iowa. You don't have to drive far before you see one on the side of the road. Sometimes they're standing still, frozen in the headlights. Sometimes they bound away in time. And sometimes... they don't. It was an understood sadness, in a completely different landscape.

But there was another reason kangaroos gathered near the roadside—a detail I never would have expected.

Out in the desert, water is scarce, and green grass is scarcer. Weeks, sometimes months, can go by without rain. The land turns dry and brittle, and food becomes harder to find. And yet, right along the edges of the road, thin strips of green would appear like small miracles.

It turns out cars—through exhaust and condensation—release enough moisture to allow grass to grow in those narrow stretches. Not much, but enough. Enough to draw in hungry kangaroos, especially during long dry spells when they're desperate for anything green.

And that's where danger and survival collide.

When drivers in Australia see a kangaroo on the side of the road, they're encouraged—if it's safe to do so—to stop and check the pouch. A mother kangaroo's pouch is incredibly strong, almost like a built-in seatbelt. Despite when the mother doesn't survive, her baby—the joey—often does.

Some joeys can survive for days inside their mother's pouch.

People are encouraged to keep pillowcases in their cars for this exact reason. A pillowcase can act as a substitute pouch—dark, enclosed, and comforting. If a joey is found, it can be gently placed inside and brought to a rescue center like the Kangaroo Sanctuary.

If the joey is young—still pink and hairless, called a "pinkie"—keeping it warm becomes critical. They can't regulate their own body temperature yet. The best thing you can do is hold them close to your body, share your warmth, and keep their world muted and dark to reduce stress.

And after rescuing the joey, there's one more difficult but important step—moving the mother off the road. Not solely out of respect, but to protect other wildlife. Animals like the wedge-tailed eagle, with wingspans stretching over nine feet, are drawn to roadkill and can easily become victims themselves as they feed too close to passing cars.

All of this—the rescues, the reality, the second chances—is what eventually brings those tiny joeys to locations like the sanctuary.

And that's where my days began.

Most days when I arrived, another American volunteer, Leah, was already there. She would give me a full update—if we had any new joeys from the previous week, who had been fed, who was sleeping, who wasn't feeling well, and if there were any new rules or changes. The joeys were usually tucked into their pouches, heads poking out of laundry baskets lined up like little nurseries. There were typically ten to twelve joeys inside, who spent most of their time indoors.

Leah would go through their names one by one. I wrote them down in order so I could remember who was who, sometimes snapping pictures to help me keep track. It wasn't easy at first. Many of them looked so similar, but over time, I learned to spot the tiny differences—the shape of their ears, a patch of lighter fur, the space between their eyes, a darker nose. Each joey was unique, and soon, each had a personality too.

Outside the door was another group—about fifteen joeys in the paddock area. Some were still bottle-fed, while others were nearly ready to move to the next stage, with less contact with humans. From there, they would, with time, move to another area where Brolga was often the only person who interacted with them. This step was crucial in preparing them for life in the bush.

There was also a separate area for the larger roos who were almost ready for release. Timing mattered. We tried to release them when it wasn't extremely hot and ideally after good rain—rare in the Red Centre—when the land would be greener and food more abundant, giving them a better chance of survival.

And there were the permanent residents. These were kangaroos who, due to injuries as joeys, would never be able to be safely released. They lived out their lives at the sanctuary and were more accustomed to human interaction. This was also the area Brolga used during tours, where visitors could learn about kangaroos up close.

Some of my favorite kangaroos lived there—Beyoncé and Disco Dave. They were two of the first kangaroos I ever cared for, and they will always have a place in my heart.

After Leah finished giving me the rundown, I usually started with chores. There were always bottles to wash. Always laundry. Towels, pouches, blankets—loads and loads of laundry. I would throw a load in, wash bottles, do dishes, and get the sanctuary ready for the next round of feeding.

One of my favorite parts of the day was taking the basket joeys outside for some sunshine. This was especially true when the weather was cooler and I didn't have to wear a fly net to keep the flies from going in my ears, nose, and mouth. I would carry the baskets out one at a time, set up my chair, and gently take each joey out to hold while they soaked in the warmth.

Those moments were pure magic.

I would sit there tuning in to the birds, surrounded by red dirt and desert, holding joey after joey. No stress. No noise. No rush. Only me, nature, and these tiny lives trusting me completely. It was during those moments when my heart felt the most at peace. Truly happy. It's a feeling I hope I never forget.

I would watch the other joeys dig little hollows in the red dirt to make their beds. Some would try so hard to stay awake, their heads slowly nodding until sleep finally won. Other joeys would come up to me and scratch for a pouch yet they were at the age they didn't need to be in their mother's pouch. Some of the joeys would put themselves to bed and jump in the laundry basket as if it was an open invitation. I held each joey, one by one, and brought them back inside.

Once inside, it was time to prepare bottles. This part required speed and focus. I often had ten to twelve joeys to feed, and they knew exactly when it was feeding time. I had to warm the water to the right temperature, mix the formula correctly, and make sure each bottle was right.

I always started with the smallest joeys. Some were so tiny their mouths were barely open and gently needed help to latch. Sometimes I would place my hand over their eyes and hold them close, mimicking the safety of their mother's pouch. It helped them relax and feed. Only a few volunteers were needed to feed them, so they became acquainted with our scent and felt safe. I respected how intentional Brolga was about this—it truly gave the joeys the best chance to grow strong and be released.

With the larger joeys inside, I could feed two at a time, sitting on the floor in front of their basket, holding up bottles like some kangaroo milk bar. Some gulped their milk down. Others took their sweet time.

After feeding, the smallest joeys needed help going to the bathroom—like their mothers would do in the wild. We would lay out a towel, gently rub their bottoms to help them pee and poop, clean them up, sometimes let them hop a little, and tuck them back into their pouches.

The older joeys outside handled their business on their own. I would bottle-feed them too—sometimes up to eight at a time. The trick was getting them all lined up and latched without crawling over each other. Once they were fed, I would show them their pouches, and they would hop right back in, ready to settle down.

Then came more cleaning—washing bottles, switching laundry, hanging clothes, folding towels, sweeping and mopping floors, and recording how much each joey ate. The work was constant, but it never felt like a burden. It felt meaningful.

One of my favorite side jobs was feeding Beatrice, the camel. Her bottle was a massive two-liter bottle, mixed with a drill-style mixer and topped with a giant nipple. Her milk smelled awful—but Beatrice made up for it with her personality.

I would take my car, Dimples, down the curvy dirt path, through a couple of gates, and every single time, Beatrice would be waiting at the fence—pacing, making those unmistakable camel sounds, ready for her bottle. She drank with such force it required me to hang on tight, so it didn't fly out of my hands. Afterward, I'd give her lots of love and scratches before heading back to the sanctuary.

At the end of the day, I would have one last round of cuddles with the joeys. Brolga would usually stop by to check on everyone, make sure all was well, and I would head home—tired, dusty, and full in the best way.

It wasn't volunteer work.

It was love.

It was a purpose.

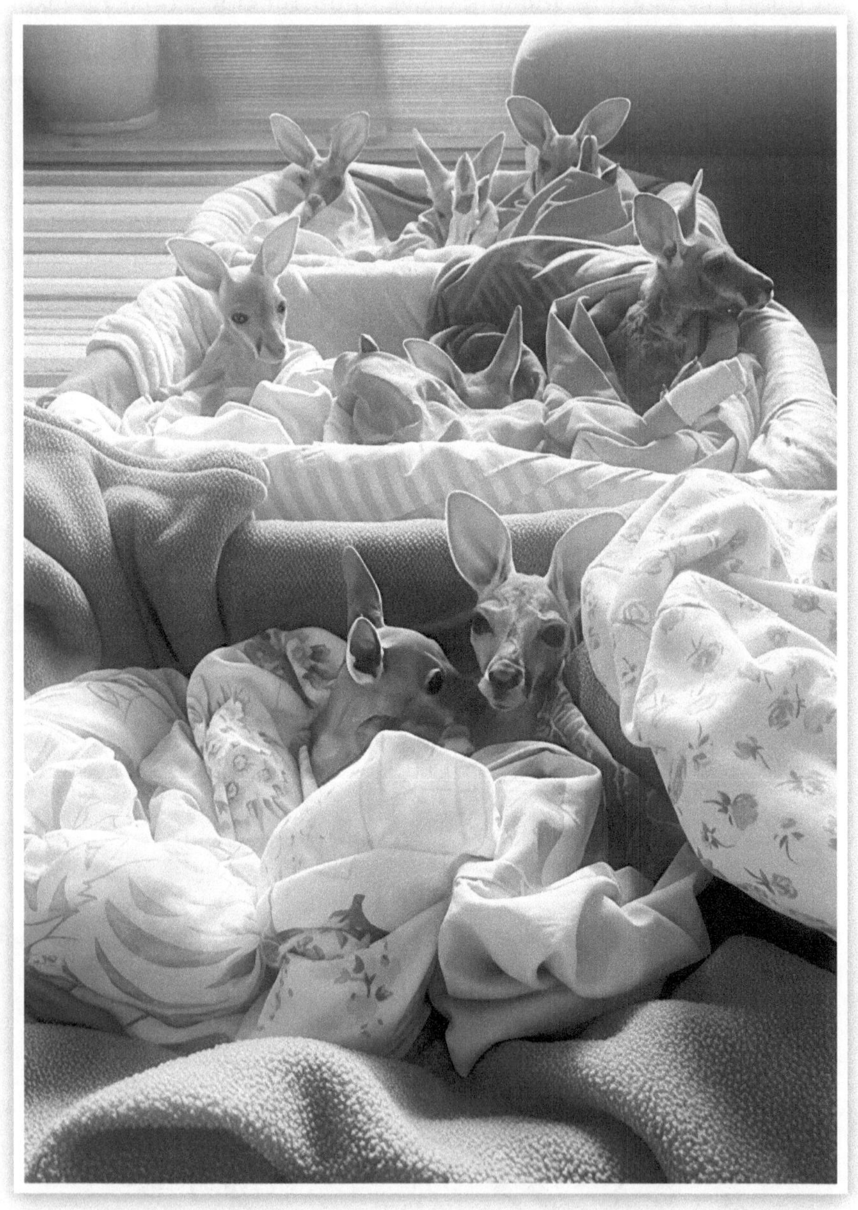

These two kangaroos visited my donga almost daily—I named them Thelma and Louise.

See the moments behind this journey.
Photos, videos, and stories from Australia and beyond: @Spacethedesertcreates
Scan to follow the journey

SPACETHEDESERTCREATES

MUCH LOVE TO THE KANGAROOS
I CARED FOR AT THE
KANGAROO SANCTUARY

1. Sylvie
2. Quantas
3. Tristan
4. Frankie
5. Samson
6. Honey Butterfly
7. Pixie
8. JoJo
9. Nate
10. Jarra
11. Disco Dave
12. Tiny Tim
13. Beyonce
14. Aaron
15. Pickles
16. Pippa
17. Mulga
18 Rodney
19. Montey
20. Aaron
21. Wobbles
22. Bella
23. Sargeant
24. Bobby
25. Taylor (Taylor Swift)
26. Biscuit
27. Connor
28. Skippy
29. Debbie
30. Mia
31. Spot
32. Margo
33. Pauline
34. Thumper
35. Stella
36. Emily
37. Jacky
38. Jumper
39. Willy
40. Spicey
41. Walu
42. Match Sticks
43. Rocky
44. Sugar
45. Anna
46. Rusty
47. Forrest
48. Sharona
49. Lucy
50. Skip
51. Charlie

AN AUSTRALIAN GLOSSARY OF SLANG

AUSTRALIAN	AMERICAN
How ya goin?	How are you?
Good on ya!	Good job!
no worries	you're welcome
have a go	try it
righto	right
dodgy	suspicious
dunny	toilet
bog	toilet
loo	toilet
dunny paper	toilet paper
drop dunny	outhouse
lollies	candy
swag	sleeping bag
torch	flashlight
bitumen	asphalt/blacktop
sunnies	sunglasses
jumper	coat
textas	markers

AUSTRALIAN	AMERICAN
arvo	afternoon
swampy/aircon	air conditioner
chook	chicken
brekky	breakfast
esky	cooler
rock melon	cantaloupe
biscuits	cookie
avo	avocado
bangers or snags	sausages
chips	French fries
tomato sauce	ketchup
fairy floss	cotton candy
sultanas	raisins
capsicum	Pepper
coriander	cilantro
pavlovas	type of dessert
postmix	fountain pop
meat pie	reminds me of a Hot Pocket
prawns	Shrimp
rubber	eraser
boot	trunk

AUSTRALIAN	AMERICAN
bonnet	hood of your car
bottle-O	gas station
grog	alcohol
runners/joggers	tennis shoes
thongs	flip flops
bum bag	don't use the word we use in the States
maths	plural form of math
zed	letter Z
tea	can be dinner
ute	truck
bush	country
bogan	redneck/hick
bloke	man
footy	football- Aussie rules
American football	NFL
grannie flat	apartment
cheeky	trouble
bathers, togs, swimmers	bathing suit
budgie smuggler	speedo
chockablock	full

AUSTRALIAN	AMERICAN
chockers (ex-It's chockers in here)	full/crowded
Chrissie	Christmas
servo	gas station
petrol	gas
paddock	field
bush walking	hike
cheer for your team	never use root
ankle bitter	small child
hoo-roo	good-bye
smoko	tea break around 10:00
CBD	Central Business District- downtown
knickers	underwear
jocs	men's underwear
holiday	vacation
lift	elevator
car park	parking lot
cinema	movie
show	state fair
fringe	bangs
pram	baby stroller

AUSTRALIAN	AMERICAN
hire	to rent something like a car
referee	references on your resume
fortnightly	every other week
pegs	clothes pins
transition	kindergarten
queue	Line
roadtrain	semitruck
trolley	shopping cart
skip	jumping rope (learned this the hard way)
verandah	porch
takeaway	to-go order
tele	TV
Maccas	McDonald's
footpath	sidewalk
cuppa	cup of tea
lappy	laptop
tucker	food found in the Outback
doona	comforter
nappy	diaper
indicator	turn signal in car- blinker

AUSTRALIAN	AMERICAN
spider	float- with pop and ice cream
tradies	jobs like a carpenter
chippy	carpenter
sparky	electrician
mozzie	mosquitos
tracky daks	sweatpants
waistcoat	vest
singlet	tank top
pissed	drunk
pissed as a fart	REALLY drunk
serviette	napkin
Kiwi	someone from New Zealand
IGA	local grocery store
biro	pen
globe	lightbulb
Boxing Day	Dec. 26th
plait	braid
hen's night	bachelorette party
Palms	people from England
Yanks	Americans
crack a tinny	open a beer

AUSTRALIAN	AMERICAN
cockie	short for cockatoo
ambo	ambulance
berko	went crazy
bloody ripper	fantastic
bloody oath	the truth
blue	to have an argument- The two blokes over there are having a blue.
brolly	umbrella
bugger	What a bugger! - frustration about something
daggy	uncool/not fashionable
dry as a dead dingo	extreme thirst
ey	a way to end a sentence - The weather is good, ey?
full stop	period at the end of a sentence
flannie	flannel shirt
oi	used to get someone's attention instead of yelling HEY
gumbies	waterproof boots
have a crack	try something
rip snorter	great, fantastic

AUSTRALIAN	AMERICAN
rock up	to turn up
hoo roo	see you later
knackered	tired
she'll be right	it'll turn out okay
off ya chops	drunk
sticky beak (my favorite)	nosing around
lollipop man	cross guard
blue whistle	pain killer
dag	funny person
having a winge	Complaining
gone walkabout	missing/ off wandering
flat out	very busy
bogged	stuck
goannas	huge lizards
shelia	woman
tinnies	cans of beer
knackered	exhausted
The Red Centre	Central Australia
station	huge cattle ranch
brumbies	wild horses

www.ingramcontent.com/pod-product-compliance
Lightning Source LLC
Chambersburg PA
CBHW051142130726
47988CB00005B/1958